A Short History of
The Sailing Ship

PLATE I

SHIP ON THE SHRINE OF ST PETER THE MARTYR, MILAN (1340)

Copyright photograph from the replica in the Victoria and Albert
Museum

[See p. 105.]

A Short History of
The Sailing Ship

Romola Anderson
and
R. C. Anderson

Dover Publications, Inc.
Mineola, New York

Bibliographical Note

This Dover edition, first published in 2003, is an unabridged republication of *The Sailing-Ship: Six Thousand Years of History*, originally published
by Robert M. McBride & Company, New York, in 1926.

Library of Congress Cataloging-in-Publication Data

Anderson, Romola.
    A short history of the sailing ship / Romola Anderson and R.C.
Anderson.—Dover ed.
        p. cm.
    Originally published: The sailing ship. New York : Robert M. McBride,
1926.
    ISBN 0-486-42988-1 (pbk.)
        1. Sailing ships—History. I. Anderson, R. C. (Roger Charles), b. 1883.
II. Title.

VM15.A623 2003
623.8'203—dc21

                                                          2003053167

Manufactured in the United States of America
Dover Publications, Inc., 31 East 2nd Street, Mineola, N.Y. 11501

PREFACE

THIS book is merely a sketch of a very large subject. Each chapter might well make a separate book, and any of those books might well be as large as this volume in which we have tried to cover the whole ground. Naturally, our attempt can at best be little more than a summary, but we hope that the summary, within its limits, is accurate and complete.

Our object has been to trace from their sources, or as near their sources as possible, the two main streams of development, the Southern and the Northern, until their junction in the fifteenth century to produce the standard European full-rigged ship. After that we have tried to give some account of the gradual improvement of that standard type, of its culmination in the clipper ships of the nineteenth century, and of its slow but inevitable decline as one trade after another was taken from it by the steamship.

We have made no attempt to deal with ships and boats of other than European peoples, except in so far as an occasional reference to some of them might help to illustrate a point nearer home. Needless to say, we have considered the whole basin of the Mediterranean as included in European waters from our point of view, and have thus stretched the term European to include the ancient Egyptians and the Phœnicians. In the same way we have included modern North American ships, because they are purely European in ancestry.

THE SAILING-SHIP

The drawings have been made, when possible, from the originals or from photographic facsimiles. Our aim has been to produce a faithful copy preserving the character of the original rather than to get an artistic effect; hence the wide variations in the style of work. With regard to the diagrams, clearness has been the sole object.

Our thanks are due in the first place to all those who have written on this subject before us and who have thus provided the material for this book. More particularly they are due to those who have helped us personally with drawings, photographs, and advice. Among them we wish to mention Rear-Admiral J. Hägg, of the Swedish Navy, Dr Jules Sottas, of Paris, Mr C. G. 't Hooft and Mr G. C. E. Crone, of Amsterdam, Sir Alan Moore, Mr H. H. Brindley, Mr R. Morton Nance, and Mr L. G. Carr Laughton.

R. A.
R. C. A.

CONTENTS

9

ILLUSTRATIONS

PLATES

THE SAILING-SHIP

DRAWINGS IN THE TEXT

ILLUSTRATIONS

13

THE SAILING-SHIP

ILLUSTRATIONS

15

THE SAILING-SHIP

CHAPTER I

FOR the earliest known pictures of ships we must turn to ancient Egypt. Not that we shall find there ships in their most primitive form—that can be done better in various out-of-the-way parts of the world at the present day—but because civilization seems to have dawned in Egypt, and it was there that men first began to make any lasting record of things around them.

Navigation in its simplest form is such a very ancient art that even in Egypt, where records of one kind and another go back for thousands of years, they take us nowhere near the first days of man's use of boats. Boat-building seems to have come before drawing, and many centuries before writing.

On Egyptian pottery which is certainly at least as old as 4000 B.C. we find designs which may possibly be meant for boats with a large number of paddles, but which look far more like walled buildings of some sort. Figures of men and birds on the same vases are quite well drawn, and it is difficult to believe that the artist who drew these would have made his boats so difficult to recognize. True, in the Middle Ages we find artists making excellent pictures of people in ships which are no better than caricatures, but in those cases the artists

17

very likely never saw a ship, whereas in Egypt the whole nation has always been so dependent on the Nile that every one must have known the appearance of boats almost as well as that of their fellow-men.

These doubtful boats are made all the more doubtful by the fact that in the same collection of pottery in the British Museum there is one specimen with quite a good picture of a sailing-boat; this shows that boats were not beyond the capacity of artists of those far-off times. On the whole, there is wonderfully little difference between this vessel (Fig. 1) and those which we shall find in Egyptian carvings of two or three thousand years later. The hull is the same shape, very round underneath and rising well out of the water for a long distance at each end. The only striking difference is that the bow is carried up very much higher than in later ships. The sail is practically the same as in all the earlier Egyptian sculptures, a square sail with a yard at the top and a boom at the bottom. The mast appears to be a single stick, but there is no indication of how it was supported or how the sail was hoisted and controlled.

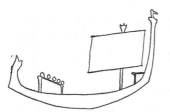

Fig. 1. EGYPTIAN BOAT
4000 B.C. or earlier

For knowledge of that sort we have to jump a thousand years or more—not such a long jump after all, when we consider that we know something of Egypt for at least six thousand years. Here, then, at a date about 3000 B.C., we have (Fig. 2) a ship carved in stone and showing quite a lot of detail. The shape of the hull is the same except that the ends are not turned right up as they were before. There are thirteen oars on each side, and there are three very large oars used for steering. The sail is higher and narrower ; it has a yard at its head and probably a boom at its foot. The mast is composed of two spars joined together at the top and set some little distance apart at the bottom. These two spars were probably not one in front of the other, but

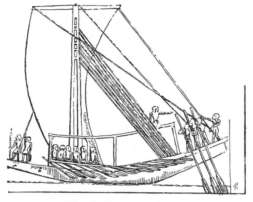

Fig. 2. EGYPTIAN BOAT
About 3000 B.C.

side by side. The Egyptian artist had a way of twisting things round when he wanted to show details that were really hidden by other parts. The ropes leading to the ship's side from the mast are no doubt shrouds to hold it up against the pull of the sail. They are taken much nearer the stern than would be done nowadays, but this is easy to explain. The ancient Egyptians never sailed unless the wind was well behind them, and in any case the ∧-shaped mast would want more support in a lengthwise direction than sideways. It has a single stay going to the bow of the ship to keep it from falling backward, and the halliard which hoisted the yard is taken from the masthead to the stern to act

THE SAILING-SHIP

as a backstay. The two ropes from the ends of the yard are braces, by means of which the sail could be turned to allow for a wind not quite over the stern.

There is no doubt that Egyptian ships as far back as 3000 B.C. were well-built vessels of considerable size. This was the beginning of the Pyramid Age, when stone was brought by water from a long way up the Nile. The first boats of the Nile Valley were probably simply floats made of reeds tied together in bundles. Something of the sort is in use even at the present time. Gradually these reed-bundle boats became more 'shipshape,' and eventually, at some very remote period, wooden boats on the same pattern were introduced. These wooden boats were very different in construction from anything that we are used to seeing to-day. Egypt is a land badly off for large timber, and the method of building by means of keel, ribs, and planks which developed elsewhere from the great canoes scooped out of a single tree was never possible, or at any rate never easy, in Egypt. That being so, the Egyptians built their boats of short, narrow pieces of wood, each pinned sideways to the next. They gave them no keel, and depended for strength on thick sides and strong fastenings. The shape of the hulls, with the great overhang at each end, was perhaps partly due to their having been copied from the reed-bundle boats and partly to its convenience for loading and unloading by running one end over the bank of the river.

Apparently the two boats shown in Fig. 3, from the same monument, belong to the two kinds of building. The lower is evidently made of some material that has to be lashed together, and the droop of its bow suggests something rather flexible, while the upper looks stiffer

20

and has no sign of lashings. There is another very important difference : the crew of the lower boat are paddling, and those of the upper one are rowing. This step from paddles to oars is quite simple when once it is thought of. All that is necessary is some kind of fixture against which the paddle can work ; it then becomes in principle an oar. Still, like many simple

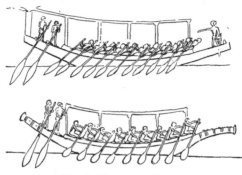

Fig. 3. EGYPTIAN BOATS
About 3000 B.C.

things, it took a long time for men to think of it, and when it was made it marked an important advance, because it allowed ships to be made much bigger than would ever have been possible with paddles.

So far we have been concerned with boats for use on the Nile. These were important because of their early date, but the true ship could be developed only in open water, and it was only by voyages across the sea that the art of shipbuilding could spread from one people to another. Now we come to real seagoing ships.

By about 3000 B.C. the Egyptians seem to have been sending ships into the Eastern Mediterranean at least as far as Crete, which lies some three hundred miles north-west from the mouth of the Nile, and the coast of Phœnicia, some two hundred miles to the north-east. About a hundred years after this we know definitely that Egyptian ships brought home cedar-wood, which they must have loaded in Phœnician harbours. A little later, about 2700 B.C., Sahure, King of Egypt, sent out a fleet of eight ships which brought back Phœnician prisoners. Representations of these ships were carved on the walls of a temple and have fortunately been preserved.

They show vessels very much like the Nile boats with certain extra fittings (Fig. 4). The enormous rope

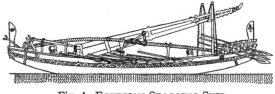

Fig. 4. EGYPTIAN SEAGOING SHIP
About 2700 B.C.

running from end to end over a row of forked posts is a truss designed to prevent the ends of the ship from dropping. This dropping of the ends, or ' hogging,' has always been a failing of wooden ships. The *Victory* has hogged about eighteen inches in the bows, and the motor-launches which were bought in such numbers from America during the War were hogging more and more as time went on. The Egyptian method of guarding against it was thoroughly practical ; something very much like it is used in shallow-draught river-steamers even to-day. The exact way in which the truss was made fast at each end is not quite clear, but it was probably taken round the middle of a heavy cross-timber, which was held in place by lashings passing

22

right underneath the ship. How it was tightened, or
' set up,' is clear enough. It was done on the principle
of the tourniquet—by putting a stick between the separate ropes that made up the truss, twisting as tightly as

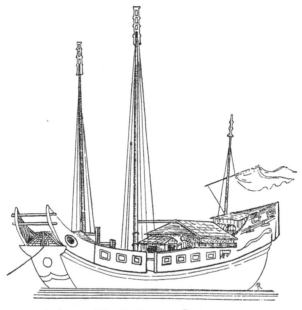

Fig. 5. CHINESE JUNK
From a drawing of about 1825

was necessary, and then lashing the end of the stick to
prevent it from untwisting. The pattern along the side
is apparently formed by two ropes with another wound
criss-cross from one to the other. It may have been
another strengthening device or perhaps only a fender
to save the sides from chafing.

A small but very important detail is the eye drawn
on the upper part of the ' stem,' the upright post in
the extreme point of the bows. This ornamental eye is

still found in many parts of the world, particularly on the Chinese ships (Fig. 5) which we call 'junks.' The ∧-shaped mast is another ancient Egyptian feature that can now be seen in the East. For instance, the ships of the Irawadi river in Burma have a mast and sail that are very like those of the Nile vessels of five thousand years ago. Some people think that these things prove that the nations of the East learned to build ships from the Egyptians, at any rate indirectly. It has even been claimed "that naval architecture is an Egyptian art, and that the main lines of the history of shipbuilding for the whole world were laid down in Egypt toward the end of the fourth millennium B.C."

This seems a very large claim. No doubt the Egyptians as leaders in the march of civilization did point out the way to more backward peoples, but it must be remembered that it is as easy to find differences as resemblances, and some of the differences are very striking. The Burmese ship may have a mast and sail that came from Egypt, but they are used in a vessel of utterly different construction from anything that was known to the Egyptians. Even the most emphatic believers in the theory that Egypt was responsible for everything have to acknowledge that it is very unlikely that the dug-out canoe was invented or used in Egypt, and yet it is the dug-out that is still the foundation of Burmese shipbuilding. In China too the way that ships are built, and have been built for many centuries, seems to have no possible connexion with anything Egyptian.

Leaving this question, which would want a large book to itself, we will return to definite facts and consider some more Egyptian seagoing ships of about 1500 B.C. Queen Hatshepsut, who was then ruler of

Egypt, wanted various rare things, particularly myrrh, from a distant country known as Punt. Where exactly Punt was is not certain ; it may have been Somaliland or it may have been a good deal farther down the east coast of Africa. In any case, the way there lay down the Red Sea, and the Queen fitted out a fleet of five

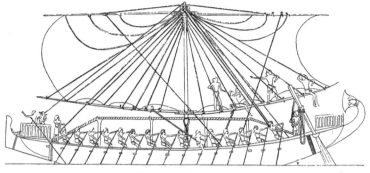

Fig. 6. EGYPTIAN SEAGOING SHIP
About 1500 B.C.

ships to go there. In those days there was a canal from the Nile to the Red Sea, so that it was as easy for ships from the Nile to go that way as across the Mediterranean. The Suez Canal was nothing new after all.

The expedition was a great success, and the Queen was so pleased with the result that she had a full account of it engraved on the walls of a temple at Deir-el-Bahari, near Thebes. Two carvings, each showing five ships, are there to this day. One shows the fleet just arriving at its destination, in the other it is about to start for home.

The ships are all alike, but they are shown under various conditions. We see them sailing and rowing at the same time (as in Fig. 6), rowing with sail lowered, and lying close to the shore loading cargo. We even see

25

the rowers in the second ship backing water to check her way as she reaches the beach. In a general way there is not very much difference between these ships of Hatshepsut and those of Sahure fifteen hundred years before. The shape of the hull is much the same, and it is strengthened with a rope truss in just the same way. In details there are many changes to notice. One of the most striking is that the double mast has been replaced by a single spar, which seems to be lashed in place in some way. There are two stays and a single backstay, while the two halliards are also taken well toward the stern. Though one would expect an ordinary mast to need shrouds more than the Λ-shaped mast did, there is no sign of them. It would seem that the mast was stepped pretty firmly in the ship, so firmly that it was not often lowered. Both the yard and the boom are made of two pieces lashed together, a practice that still survives in ships of the Mediterranean and Red Sea. From the masthead to the yard there run eight ropes. When the yard is hoisted only two of them are tight; the others hang down loosely. With the yard down, they are all drawn tight. No less than sixteen similar ropes run from the masthead to the boom. It is difficult to see the purpose of all these ropes, but it seems clear that one pair of those on the yard were ' lifts ' intended to keep the yard horizontal, or to tilt it up at one end if required. Two braces are shown on the yard, and two on the boom ; the latter are so near the middle that they may have been used more for keeping the boom down than for twisting it round.

The steering-gear shows a great advance. It is no longer an oar but a real rudder. A steering-oar is held actually in the hand of the helmsman and can be pushed about in any direction, but a rudder is secured in such a way that it can only be twisted in its socket, and has a tiller, or projecting handle, which the helmsman holds. These rudders, one on each side, were secured in two places : to the side of the ship and to a post rising well above the side a trifle farther forward.

Beneath the rowers there is a row of oblong marks on the hull. At first sight these look like ports, or holes, for a second row of oars, but they are really the ends of the beams which supported the deck and held the ship's sides together. The bow is very like that of Sahure's ships, but the great lotus-flower in the stern is a new feature.

The size of the actual ships is uncertain. If they are drawn on a scale of 1:14 (2 digits = 1 cubit), which seems a probable scale since the Egyptian cubit contained 28 digits, they would be about 88 feet long, and their oars would be about $3\frac{1}{2}$ feet apart. The ships of Sahure would seem to have been about 60 feet long.

Another scene in the sculptures of Deir-el-Bahari shows an enormous vessel being towed down the Nile with two great obelisks on board. The two obelisks put up by Hatshepsut were much bigger than the one on the Thames Embankment in London which we call ' Cleopatra's Needle.' They were about 100 feet long and weighed about 350 tons each. We know from an inscription that the vessel used to bring down two smaller obelisks had been 207 feet long and 69 feet wide. Much of the inscription relating to the transport of this second pair of obelisks has been destroyed, but what there is certainly suggests that another, bigger vessel was built. Such as it is, it runs as follows : ". . . trees in all the land to build a very great boat enlarging . . . to load two obelisks at Elephantine." The two obelisks end to end as shown would require a length of 200 feet or more, and they would certainly have to be carried without bearing on the part of the hull which was out of the water at each end. If the drawing is in proportion—as it seems to be, except for the size of some of the men—the ship must have been at the very least 300 feet long, and more probably about 330. It was evidently of the same general shape as the ships which went to Punt, but it has three rows of beams showing. These must have been connected with one another and with the deck on which the obelisks lay by means of pillars, or 'stanchions,' otherwise the lower beams would have been of no use in helping to take the weight. No less than thirty rowing-boats were used to tow the enormous 'lighter' down the river.

It is worth noting that this vessel was very much bigger than the largest wooden sailing warship ever built. As for the actual loading and unloading of the obelisks, it is a mystery how it was managed without steam or hydraulic power and without even pulleys and wire ropes. When Cleopatra's Needle was brought to London an iron cylinder was built round it as it lay, and was then rolled down to the river with the obelisk inside. After that a deck-house was added, and the whole thing was towed to England by a steamer. The Egyptian method may not have been quite so ingenious, but it was evidently thoroughly efficient.

By the time of Hatshepsut other nations besides the Egyptians were beginning to take a share in the navigation of the Eastern Mediterranean. The Phœnicians had not yet reached their prime, but the people of the Greek islands, and especially of Crete, were in a high state of civilization by 2000 B.C. and had fine ships of a pattern quite different from those of Egypt. Unfortunately, Cretan artists have not left us such good pictures of ships as the Egyptians. Apparently there were two quite distinct kinds of ships : the ' long ship,' meant mainly for rowing, and the ' round ship,' meant mainly for sailing. Among the Egyptians this difference does not seem to have been made, but from the Cretans onward it can be traced through Greek and Roman ships down almost to the end of wooden ships.

The long type was a good deal straighter in the line of the hull than the Egyptian vessels ; it had a stern that turned upward suddenly and rose high above the water, while its bow rose very little. It was rowed by a large number of oars and steered by big steering-oars or side-rudders. Mast and sail are not shown. One new feature appears very clearly, both in designs on pottery and in clay models; this is the pointed ' ram bow,' meant for smashing holes in the sides of enemies' ships. From now on we shall find this ram bow as an invariable feature of the Mediterranean long ship, or galley. In the round-ship type there is always a mast and very often no oars. The two ends are more alike, and the whole shape of the hull is more like that of Egyptian ships of the time.

Soon after the days of the Punt expedition some of the Greek islands, perhaps Crete itself, were subject to the King of Egypt, whose power extended also through the whole of Palestine and Syria. This state of affairs did not last very long, for other nations began to press in from the north, and soon Crete was overrun by the ancestors of the Greeks of classical times, while the Hittites from Asia Minor began to advance into Syria. Driven out by the Greeks, the Cretans tried to find another home, and, in spite of being defeated at sea by the Egyptians, some of them managed to establish themselves in the south of Palestine, where we know them as the Philistines of the Bible.

The carving in which Rameses III, the last great ruler of the Egyptian Empire, celebrated his defeat of these " Northern People " in about 1200 B.C. shows quite distinct types of ships in the two fleets. The

Fig. 7. EGYPTIAN WARSHIP
About 1200 B.C.

Egyptian ships (Fig. 7) are of the same shape as before, but they have changed in details almost everywhere. The stern has lost its lotus decoration and ends in a thin, upturned point, while the bow has now a lion's head right on the end of the actual hull. The rowers are protected by bulwarks, and there is a ' top ' at the masthead ; these two features would perhaps be found only in warships. The sail has changed too ; it has lost the boom at its foot, and it can now be furled beneath the yard while the yard is still hoisted.

The northern ships (Fig. 8) are apparently pure sailing-ships. They are alike at bow and stern, and have comparatively straight hulls, with the ends turning up very suddenly and finishing with birds' heads as decoration. Their masts and sails are exactly like those of the Egyptians, but it must be remembered

30

that they are drawn by an Egyptian artist, who might easily overlook small differences and draw the rig to which he was accustomed.

This battle was one of the last successes of the Egyptian Empire. Egypt was to exist as an independent country for several centuries yet, but as a great power in the world she was finished. Within the next century the Philistines, the Hebrews, and the

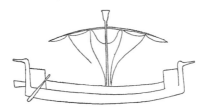

Fig. 8. CRETAN WARSHIP
About 1200 B.C.

Aramæans had taken from her the whole of Syria and Palestine. At the same time the Egyptians, who had never been a seafaring people by nature, were replaced as the traders of the Levant by the Phœnicians, one of the greatest maritime nations of history.

On the whole, ships seem to have changed very little in the course of the last two or three thousand years. Egypt may have led the world in civilization, and in consequence may have had much to do with the early stages of shipbuilding and navigation, but for some reason Egyptian shipbuilding settled down into a groove, and it was left to other nations to introduce anything in the way of new departures. This had been begun already by the Cretans; it was carried very much farther by the Phœnicians and by their successors, the Greeks and Romans.

CHAPTER II

PHŒNICIA, GREECE, AND ROME
1000 B.C.–A.D. 400

WITH the fall of the Egyptians and Cretans their place at sea was taken by the Phœnicians, for at the moment the Greeks were too new to the sea to be very important. Though we know a great deal about the doings of the Phœnicians at sea, both as traders and as fighters, we know next to nothing of their ships. Apart from a few coins, they have left us no representations of their own ships, and the little we know is based simply on the work of Egyptian and Assyrian artists. Now, when we are dealing with a time when communication from one country to another was still something of an event, it is dangerous to take an artist of one country as a reliable guide to the appearance of the ships of another. He might possibly have happened to be there when the strangers arrived, but he was far more likely to have to work from his knowledge of the ships of his own people, with perhaps a few hints from his friends in the seaport towns.

For this reason it will not do to lay too much stress on the resemblance between the Phœnician ships shown on an Egyptian carving of about 1500 B.C. and Egyptian ships of the same date. Certainly the Phœnicians show no oars and have a sort of open-work fence along their decks to protect their cargo, but otherwise, both in hull and rig, they are purely

Egyptian. Of course, it is quite possible that Phœnician ships of this date may have been copied from Egyptian patterns, but this can hardly be proved from one solitary example.

The next representation of a Phœnician ship (Fig. 9) comes from an Assyrian sculpture of about 700 B.C. It shows ships employed in the timber trade, and suggests

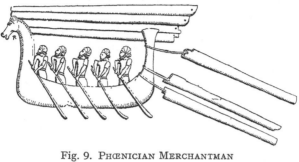

Fig. 9. PHŒNICIAN MERCHANTMAN
About 700 B.C.

that besides the timber that was actually loaded in the ship some was towed in the form of rafts. This is exactly what we should expect from the account in the Bible of the arrangements for the supply of timber for Solomon's temple some two hundred and fifty years earlier. Hiram, King of Tyre, the chief of the Phœnician cities, wrote to Solomon, saying : " I will do all thy desire concerning timber of cedar, and concerning timber of fir. My servants shall bring them down from Lebanon unto the sea : and I will convey them by sea in floats unto the place that thou shalt appoint me, and will cause them to be discharged there." Timber in rafts or floats could hardly be taken from place to place by sea unless it was towed by ships, and the ships would certainly be loaded as well.

THE SAILING-SHIP

Apart from their cargo, there is nothing very noticeable about these ships except the figureheads in the shape of horses. These do seem to have been a feature of one kind of Phœnician ship, not only those from the home ports, but even ships from the cities founded by the Phœnicians at Carthage on the north coast of Africa and at Cadiz in Spain. There is a story that about 112 B.C. such a figurehead was found washed up in East Africa and was considered by seafaring men to belong to a ship from Cadiz. This has been taken as a proof that the Phœnician colonists at Cadiz had gone far enough to round the Cape and sail the waters of the Indian Ocean. It may be so, but after all we know that Solomon had a fleet in the Red Sea manned in part by Phœnicians and no doubt built on Phœnician designs, and it is possible that Phœnician influence lingered long in those waters.

Solomon and Hiram in partnership traded with Ophir, somewhere in the south of Arabia, and with Tarshish, in the south-west of Spain. The Phœnicians alone went much farther ; they certainly went to Brittany and Cornwall and may conceivably have reached the Baltic. This has been suggested as an explanation of the similarity in appearance between the ships of the Vikings and those of the Phœnicians, as far as we know anything of them, but it can hardly be said to be more than a remote possibility.

In the other direction the Carthaginians explored the African coast as far as Cape Verde or thereabouts in 460 B.C. and had a trading-station near Cape Blanco, some fifteen hundred miles beyond the Straits of Gibraltar. There is also a story told by Herodotus that in about 600 B.C. Necho, King of Egypt, sent out a fleet of ships with Phœnician crews from one of his Red Sea ports, and that after a voyage of more than two years they returned to Egypt by way of the Mediterranean, thus anticipating Vasco da Gama by more than two thousand years. Many people disbelieve this,

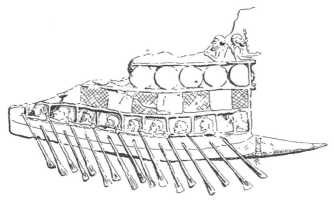

Fig. 10. PHŒNICIAN WARSHIP
About 700 B.C.

but there seems no good reason why it should not be true.

Another Assyrian sculpture of about 700 B.C. (Figs. 10 and 11) gives us an idea of the appearance of Phœnician warships. In this case it seems that the artist was really acquainted with his subject, for coins of Sidon, another of the Phœnician cities, show exactly the same type of ship (Fig. 12). These coins are some two hundred and fifty or three hundred years later, but there is no reason why ships should have changed very much, and in any case it is easy enough to find instances where ships on coins were quite as much out of date.

Clearly these Phœnician warships, if they owed anything to foreign designs, were indebted to Crete rather than Egypt. Their hulls have just the characteristics

35

that are most marked in the very unsatisfactory drawings of Cretan galleys—low bows, high sterns, a comparatively straight appearance, and a ram. The sail is that of the battle of 1200 B.C., with no boom and a ' standing ' yard. The most important thing about them is undoubtedly the arrangement of their oars at two different levels. For the moment we must leave

Fig. 11. PHŒNICIAN WARSHIP
About 700 B.C.

Fig. 12. PHŒNICIAN WARSHIP
About 400 B.C. From a coin
of Sidon

the question of how the actual rowers were disposed and simply note the fact that this is a very early instance of what would have been called later a ' bireme.'

Turning now to Greek ships, we find ourselves involved almost at once in one of the most difficult and at the same time the most interesting of all the problems connected with the ships of past ages. Put in a very few words it is this : How were the oars and the rowers of Greek and Roman galleys arranged ? At one time the ideas on this subject might have been summed up in the words " One man one theory." Recent discoveries have produced a little more agreement, but there are still many doubtful points. What follows must be taken as no more than an attempt to state one set of views with an occasional effort to explain why those views should be thought more likely to be right than others.

We are concerned now simply with the long ship, or galley, meant for fighting as a rowing vessel, and carrying sail only for use in making long passages with a fair wind. This type of ship had been developed by the Cretans and their kinsmen on the Greek mainland long before the real Greeks arrived. Some idea of what these early galleys looked like may be got from the

Fig. 13. GREEK WARSHIP
About 800–700 B.C.   From a vase

upper drawing in Fig. 34 from a vase of about 1300 B.C. When the Greeks began to take to the sea they used galleys of very much the same kind—that is to say, long, open boats with a ram bow and a high stern, and with a sort of ' flying deck ' running from end to end over the heads of the rowers. The top drawing in Fig. 33 shows the general appearance of such a galley, and Fig. 13 shows how the rowers were arranged. These are ships of about 800–700 B.C. Quite often there appear to be rowers on the upper deck as well, and in one case there are two flying decks, each with rowers on it, but this is probably simply the artist's attempt to get in the rowers of both sides.

THE SAILING-SHIP

Such galleys as these were rowed by fifty men at most, twenty-five on each side. It was not possible to go much beyond this, because too great length in a boat of such light construction simply meant that she would break in half in any sea. To get more power it was necessary to arrange more rowers in the same length. This could be done in several ways. What seems to us the obvious method—making the oars longer, and putting two or more men on each—seems never to have been the fashion in Greece. Another way would be to have a second lot of rowers right above the first; this is what is shown on some of the early vases, but it meant a rather unstable craft and very long oars for the upper rowers, and it seems also to have been discarded. A third method, having a pair of oars at the same level and almost touching one another, but making the oar nearer the stern longer than the other, and putting the two rowers side by side on the same bench, is what was done in Mediterranean galleys in the fourteenth and fifteenth centuries A.D. It was probably done now and then in ancient Greek galleys, and some people still say that it was the general rule, but this idea is almost certainly wrong. The fourth way, the way shown in the Phœnician warship of 700 B.C., and in a Greek galley of about 500 B.C. (Fig. 14), was to put the two rows of oars at different levels, and to have the holes for the lower row about half-way between those for the upper row. In this case the difference of level need only be enough to let the oars of the upper row clear the heads of the men on the lower row. The upper lot of rowers would naturally have the longer oars, and this would let them sit far enough from the side of the ship to leave room for the hands of the lower men between their legs and the ship's side.

So far so good. Unfortunately, we have to allow not only for biremes, or double-oared ships, but also for ' triremes ' ' quadriremes,' ' quinqueremes,' and (if we are to believe accounts that have come down to us)

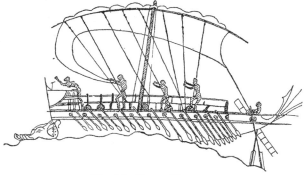

Fig. 14. GREEK BIREME
About 500 B.C.

for classes up to ' forty-remes.' It is hard to say how far it would be possible to extend the principle of one row of oar-ports above another and one man to an oar, but it is quite obvious that it would be bound to break down fairly early in the series.

We have seen that biremes were in use in Phœnicia in 700 B.C., and it is probable that they were introduced in Greece about that date. Thucydides tells us that the Corinthians invented some new kind of ship in about 700, and also that they were the first people to build triremes, or triple-oared craft, but it seems that he is speaking of two separate inventions. It is said that triremes were used in Egypt about 600, and in any case they were in general use in the Eastern Mediterranean before 500 B.C. They were the vessels with which the

39

great battles of the Persian and the Peloponnesian wars were fought.

Very many people have tried to reconstruct a Greek trireme on paper, or even in a full-sized model. Some of the attempts have been absurd, some possible but unlikely, and some quite like what the original must have been. All recent attempts agree in one very important point : the uppermost row of oars worked against the outer edge of a long, straight, overhanging structure projecting from the ship's side. They agree also that the second row worked against the upper edge of the real side of the ship, and that the third row came through holes in the side quite low down. The men on the middle row of oars sat a little nearer the side of the ship than those on the highest row. These two rows were in fact arranged exactly as already described in the fourth possible method of constructing a bireme. The men belonging to the lowest row sat exactly under those of the top row, and the ' outrigger ' allowed their oars to be long enough to reach well clear of the others. This outrigger, called in the Middle Ages the ' apostis,' was a feature of the Mediterranean galley for more than two thousand years, from classical times to the coming of steam, or, in other words, from Xerxes to Napoleon.

Considering what a great amount of Greek art has been preserved, it is extraordinary how badly off we are for representations of triremes. There are, in fact, only two about which we can feel at all certain. One is a fragment of sculpture from the Acropolis in Athens (Fig. 15). All it shows is some twenty-five feet of the middle part of the galley, but for this part it is really first-class evidence. The top row of oars is very clearly shown.

The only doubtful point is whether they are meant to pass over or under the uppermost of the four thick horizontal bands. In any case the two top bands are

Fig. 15. GREEK TRIREME
About 400 B.C.

certainly meant to represent the outrigger, or apostis. Directly below the points where these uppermost oars cross the upper band of the apostis the third row of oars can be seen coming out, just above the lowest of the four horizontal bands. Between these oars and those

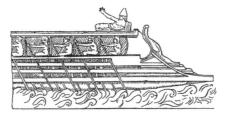

Fig. 16. BOW OF GREEK TRIREME
Pozzo drawing

of the first row the middle oars are shown coming out from under the apostis. The other diagonal lines which do not reach the water must be meant for supports for the apostis, and the two lowest horizontal bands must be ' wales,' or strips of extra-thick planking to strengthen the hull.

A drawing from an unknown original (Fig. 16) shows

41

something so very much the same that it seems possible that it may have been made from another fragment of the same sculpture. In this case the top row of oars clearly comes between the two horizontal timbers of the apostis. The bottom row is meant to be shown in the

Fig. 17. STERN OF GREEK GALLEY

same way as in the other example, but the middle row has gone astray somehow. Perhaps the carving was worn, and the artist could not make out its details quite as clearly as he would like us to believe.

The heavy ram bow is shown well in this drawing, and is confirmed by other representations on coins and elsewhere. For the stern we can turn to another carving (Fig. 17), which also shows the apostis and the steering-oar very well. Some of the buildings on deck seem rather unlikely, and it is possible that they are not meant to be part of the ship at all. This particular galley does not seem to be a trireme, but a bireme with her oars in pairs at the same level, on the third of the possible methods already mentioned. Another case of a bireme of this sort can be seen in the pedestal of the statue of *Victory* from Samothrace, now in the Louvre in Paris (Fig. 18). This is a piece of evidence of the greatest importance, because it shows in the solid things which we know otherwise only in the flat. The fore ends of the two outriggers are clearly shown, and on each side we can see the ports for the first pair of oars. They are not exactly at the same level—the fore end of the after port just overlaps the after end of the fore port—but they are so close together that it seems likely that the two oarsmen sat side by side on the same bench. In each

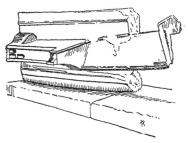

Fig. 18. Bow of Greek Galley
About 300 B.C.

port we can see the 'thole pin' against which the oars worked. Mr C. Torr in his *Ancient Ships* says that what we have called the outriggers are really 'catheads' for carrying the anchors. He refers to the idea that they are the ends of the outriggers, and says that "there is not any evidence of that." The evidence is simple enough: they look like outriggers, and they have the oar-ports that would be found in the outriggers. Mr Torr has to explain these ports as some arrangement for securing the anchor, and it would be far more reasonable to say that there is no evidence of *that*.

The *Victory* of Samothrace belongs to about 300 B.C., and by then the Greeks were no longer the most important seafaring nation of the Mediterranean. This place had been taken by the Phœnician colony of Carthage in North Africa, and was soon to be taken in turn by Rome. Two great wars called the Punic Wars were necessary to decide whether Rome or Carthage should be mistress of the sea, and it is the galleys of the third century B.C., in which these wars were fought, that have now to be considered.

By 300 B.C. the trireme had been superseded by vessels of more powerful types. Some quadriremes and quinqueremes had been built by the Greeks of Syracuse in Sicily soon after 400, and the Athenians had taken them up about 330 B.C. Very soon there were galleys of all classes up to about ' fifteen-remes.'

Now it is necessary to consider what these classes meant, and how their rowers were arranged. For the trireme the matter was fairly simple, since every one agrees that she had one man to one oar, and it is only a matter of arranging these men and their oars in a way that seems reasonably possible and that agrees with such evidence as there is. With the coming of these ' many-banked ' galleys the subject becomes far more difficult. It is admitted by every one who has studied the subject that they cannot have been produced simply by adding row after row of oars above one another. Such a thing might be possible up to about five rows, but beyond that it is simply incredible. One idea is that a ten-banked ship had ten men on an oar, and so on. Another is that after the stage of five rows of oars had been reached the method of classification changed altogether, and it was the number of sets of five oars each that was counted.

A more reasonable theory is that galleys were classed by the number of men on each set of oars. For instance,

44

a trireme's oars were arranged in sets of three, with one man to each oar. Suppose two men were put to each of the oars in the top row, then there would be four men in each set, and the vessel would be a quadrireme. Add another man on each of the middle oars, and the result is a quinquereme, with five men to a set of oars. On some such system as this it is possible to go about as far as six-banked ships with only three rows of oars, ten- or eleven-banked ships with four rows, and fifteen- or sixteen-banked ships with five rows. Beyond this it is not likely that practical seagoing ships ever went ; in fact, Livy calls a Macedonian ship of sixteen banks in 197 B.C. " useless on account of her size."

The Carthaginians were by nature a seafaring people whose whole existence depended on the sea. The Romans on the other hand were a military power— a power that was growing and that found Carthage in its way. They had little or no sea-knowledge and very few ships ; in fact, it was not until the first war had been going on for four years that they made any attempt to meet the enemy at sea. Both sides used quinqueremes as their principal fighting-ships, and the Romans, anxious to give their soldiers a chance to make up for the lack of skill of their sailors, invented the ' corvus,' a kind of boarding-bridge, which in the end proved most successful.

A French historian tells a good story, which may or may not be true. Hannibal, grandfather of the great Hannibal, met the Roman fleet, saw that they carried a new appliance of some kind, but held them in such contempt that he attacked carelessly, lost several ships, and had to fly with the rest of his fleet. Getting back to Carthage before anyone knew of his defeat, he sent an officer to say that the Romans had a fleet at sea. He pointed out that it was their first appearance and that they were quite unused to the sea, but mentioned that their ships carried certain machines of unknown use. Finally he asked whether he should attack them or not. Naturally he was told to attack, and thereupon he explained that he had already done so and had been defeated. Many times the Romans lost their fleets through pure lack of seamanship, and each time they were replaced. In the end their perseverance was rewarded, and the Carthaginian supremacy was destroyed.

Probably it was during this war that a change in the design of galleys was introduced. Such is the opinion of a recent German writer on the subject, and his account seems quite reasonable. The change was that the lowest row of oars was done away with altogether and the other two rows were given two or three men each. This allowed a quinquereme on the new system to be much lighter and handier than the old type. Probably the new style of building was what was called the Liburnian method. The two kinds seem to have gone on side by side for a long time, till the battle of Actium in 31 B.C. finally settled the superiority of the more handy type.

A carving from the temple of Fortuna at Præneste, built by Augustus after his victory at Actium, shows a large galley (Fig. 19) built on the Liburnian principle. She has been described as a bireme, but she is almost certainly of a much higher class than that. There can be very little doubt that what some writers have believed to be merely decoration along the upper part of the outrigger is really the blades of the uppermost row or rows of oars. Whether there were one or two rows here is impossible to say ; one seems most likely, but in that case the artist has put in just twice too many oar-blades. The two lowest rows are arranged just as one would expect : the lowest coming out above the true side of the ship, and the row above working

Fig. 19. ROMAN GALLEY
About 30 B.C.

through ports in the lower side of the outrigger. Probably there would be two men on each of the oars of the two lowest rows, and perhaps three on the uppermost oars. Thus, if there is really only one row working on the upper part of the outrigger the vessel would be a septereme, or sevenfold galley.

The Greeks and Romans did what the Cretans had done before them, but what the Egyptians had never done : they drew a hard and fast line between the fighting-ship which was moved by oars, and the merchantman which depended on sails. Galleys no doubt had sails, a square sail amidships and perhaps another,

47

THE SAILING-SHIP

very much smaller, right forward, and merchantmen may
have used oars occasionally ; still, speaking generally,
the distinction was quite definite. In hull too there
had been a great difference from very early days. The
galley, built for speed and for fighting, was long and
thin ; the merchantman was short and fat.

Greek artists have left us very little evidence of
the appearance of their merchantmen. Evidently the

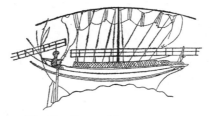

Fig. 20. GREEK MERCHANTMAN
About 500 B.C.

galley's more graceful shape and more picturesque em-
ployment made a greater appeal to them. One example
of a merchantman of about 500 B.C. (Fig. 20) comes from
the same vase as Fig. 14 and illustrates the difference
between the long ship and the round ship very well
indeed. It shows a vessel higher and deeper for her
length than the galley, with a single big square sail and
no sign of oars. Like all ancient ships, she is steered by
a pair of rudders on either side of the stern, but her
bow has a thoroughly modern look and would not be
out of place on a steam yacht. The pattern above the
side amidships is probably intended for some sort of
temporary protection to the cargo, such as was mentioned in discussing the Egyptian picture of Phœnician
merchantmen. The purpose of the long ladder-like
arrangement is not so clear ; perhaps it represents

something in the nature of an awning. The shorter
ladder in the stern is no doubt the gangway for use
when in harbour.

Roman merchantmen look heavier, but this may
only be because our knowledge of them comes from
sculpture instead of from painting. Two of the best

Fig. 21. ROMAN MERCHANTMAN
About A.D. 50

examples are shown in Figs. 21 and 22, from a tomb of
about A.D. 50 at Pompeii and from a carving of about
A.D. 200 found at Ostia, the Roman port at the mouth
of the Tiber. In a general way they agree very well.
Both show ships with high sterns and comparatively
low bows, with a mast amidships carrying a big square
sail, and a smaller mast sloping over the bows. This
mast, we know from other sources, could set a small
square sail called the ' artemon.' The later ship is
specially valuable for the details of its rigging. It
shows the setting-up of the stay and the shrouds, and
the highly developed system of ' brails ' for gathering
up the sail, each passing through a number of rings

49

sewn to the sail. It also shows a new feature in the triangular topsail that could be set above the mainsail in light winds. Another ship in the same carving has no sail set, and this lets us see the masthead with

Fig. 22. ROMAN MERCHANTMAN
About A.D. 200

the large square block of wood through which went the ropes for hoisting the yard. This we shall find in Mediterranean ships for another thirteen hundred years or so.

It was in such a ship as this, probably rather more than a hundred feet long, that St Paul made the voyage on which he was shipwrecked at Malta. The height of the stern explains why they anchored by the stern instead of by the bow. The ' rudder-bands ' that were loosened before running for the beach were the ropes which hauled the rudders out of the water. It can easily be understood that the rudders could not have been left down and loose while the ship was anchored by the stern in a heavy sea. The Bible, or at least the Authorized Version, says that they set the " mainsail "

Fig. 23. ROMAN MERCHANTMAN
About A.D. 200

to run the ship ashore. This is a mistake in translation ; the word is " artemon," and that meant the foresail set on the small mast right over the bows and used to keep the ship before the wind. Usually this was quite a small sail meant to help the steering more than to drive the ship, but sometimes it seems to have had its mast farther aft and to have been almost as big as the mainsail. Such is the case in the vessel in Fig. 23 from a carving of about A.D. 200 found at Utica, near Carthage. This is a real two-masted ship, and the two sails would be of practically equal importance.

For a good idea of a Mediterranean merchantman of about A.D. 50 one cannot do better than study the model that has been made by a distinguished French nautical archæologist, Dr Jules Sottas (Plate II). With the aid not only of the three carvings that we have shown, but of many others of varying importance, and with the story of St Paul's last voyage before him, he has made a model which certainly gives a very perfect representation of a ship of the time.

Of how these ancient Mediterranean ships were actually put together we cannot say very much. For the Phœnicians we know nothing at all, and for Greece and Rome we have to depend on casual references in literature. Their ships seem to have been built with a keel and ribs, as ships are still built to-day, and had no resemblance in this respect to the ships of ancient Egypt. It is sometimes said that they had neither stem nor sternpost, and that the keel curved up at the ends as far as the deck level. In the sense that there was no sudden angle at the ends of the keel this is true, but it can hardly be claimed that the whole keel, including the curves at each end, was a single piece of wood, and it is almost certain that the curved parts would be separate from the straight keel that joined them. They would thus be really a stem and sternpost, even if they had no special names apart from the keel. The planking was put on ' carvel-fashion,' with the edge of one plank right against the edge of the next, not overlapping, as in Northern ' clinker-built ' vessels. To hold two planks together wooden tongues were let into both of them and then held with wooden pins driven through the planks. To fasten the planks to the ribs bronze nails were used.

Some of these details can still be seen in the fragment of a Roman vessel that was found in digging the foundations for the London County Council Hall on the south side of the Thames at Westminster Bridge and that is now preserved in the London Museum. We call her Roman, because she was evidently the work of Roman builders and because coins found in her show that she dates from about A.D. 270, when Britain was under Roman rule, but there is no certainty as to where she was built or as to the purpose for which she was used. Some people think she was a fighting galley, others that she was merely a Thames ferry. Whatever she was, there was some fine workmanship put into her. Whether any of the Northern peoples could have done such good work is a doubtful question. Most people would say at once that they could not, but we shall see in the next chapter that Cæsar met Northern ships which filled him with admiration, and the ships to which he was accustomed were probably not so very inferior to this example that has so fortunately been preserved.

CHAPTER III

NORTHERN SHIPS BEFORE THE ROMANS

IT is a remarkable fact that, apart from ships still actually in use, the farther we go back from our own days the more we know of Northern shipping from actual remains. For the eighteenth century the *Victory* is almost our only direct evidence. Between her date and the days of the Vikings the known remains of ships might be counted on the fingers of one hand : for the Viking period we should have to use both hands ; for earlier days still quite an imposing list might be made.

To some extent this must be due to the fact that remains of very early vessels would have had more time to get deeply buried before natural changes and the increase of cultivation and of building made it likely that they would be disturbed. Their smaller size would have the same effect. Again, the fact that they were made of a single log of wood naturally gave them more chance of being preserved in recognizable condition than the more complicated, and therefore more fragile, vessels of later times. Whatever the reason for this survival of very early craft, it is a fortunate thing, since it gives us first-hand evidence for vessels of which we should otherwise know little or nothing.

Without going deeply into the question of how or where men first began to transport themselves by water without swimming, it is safe to say that there are at least four distinct kinds of primitive craft : the reed-bundle boat, the coracle, or skin boat, the raft, and the dug-out canoe. All of these may still be found in use in various parts of the world. The first is not likely to have been used to any great extent in the North, because of the lack of really suitable material, but the dug-out and the coracle were certainly in use before the Roman invasion.

Naturally it is the dug-outs that have been preserved. No doubt these began as simple logs on which

Fig. 24. THE BRIGG BOAT

the earliest navigators sat. Finding by accident that a hollow log would carry more than a sound one of the same size, or perhaps copying some other hollow object that floated well, men began to scoop out logs, and thus produced dug-outs such as they still use in most primitive countries.

One of the finest specimens of a Northern European dug-out that has yet been discovered was found in 1886 at Brigg in Lincolnshire and is now in the Museum at Hull (Fig. 24). When found, before it began to warp and shrink as the wood dried, it was about 48 feet long and 4 feet 6 inches wide. The oak-tree from which it was made must have been quite 6 feet thick and nearly 50 feet from the ground to its lowest branches—much bigger than any that grow in this country now. Probably it had become partly hollow from decay. The lower end of the trunk, quite close to the root, was used for the stern, and the builders went just beyond the first two branches for the bow. These two branches left knots, which fell out and made it necessary to cut plugs for the holes.

At the bow the tree was sound enough to let the boat be finished off by leaving the wood as it was, but at the stern she had to be closed off by a separate board, which fitted into a groove cut all round the part hollowed out

Fig. 25. STERN OF THE BRIGG BOAT

(Fig. 25). The joint was packed, or 'caulked,' with moss, and two holes were cut in the projecting sides of the boat to take a lashing which would hold the sides together and thus keep the stern-board in place. Other holes were cut along the sides, and by means of lashings through these and cross-pieces of wood between them the sides were prevented from falling either inward or outward.

Either from an accident or from a natural crack in the tree there was a split on one side of the boat. The way in which this had been repaired is perhaps the most interesting point about this Brigg boat. Having nothing in the way of nails or bolts, these early shipwrights worked up a thick piece of wood into the shape shown in Fig. 26, something like the wooden part of a black-lead brush with three handles instead of one. They put this on the outside of the boat with the handles through the crack, caulked the joint with moss, stuck wooden pins through the handles on the inside to hold the patch firmly in place, and finally sewed the whole thing to the boat with leather thongs passing through small holes bored through the boat and all round the edge of the patch. With the same tools and materials it would be difficult to think of a better way of doing the job.

Canoes of very much the same kind have been found

in many places, particularly at Glasgow and at Bremen in Germany. Most of them are much smaller than the Brigg boat, being about ten or fifteen feet long, or even less. Two that come near her in size are those found in the Valermoor Marsh in Schleswig-Holstein in 1878 and in Loch Arthur near Dumfries in 1876. The second of these and many of the smaller specimens have the same type of stern as the Brigg boat, while the Valer-

Fig. 26. PATCH FROM THE BRIGG BOAT

moor boat has the same kind of patch to mend a crack. This boat had ribs added inside to strengthen her.

The carrying power of a dug-out is not very great. The ordinary shape of a tree-trunk makes it impossible to make them very deep, and the thickness of their sides makes them heavy for their size. In anything like rough water, either on a lake or on the sea, they must have shipped a lot of water. To get over this difficulty men hit on the idea of lashing or pegging an extra piece of wood along the side. When once this had been done it would be a simple step to add a second strip. Later on, as tools improved and it became easier to cut or split wood into pieces of any size required, the planking grew and the original dug-out shrank till it was nothing more than a heavy keel, and the true plank-built boat came into existence. Examples of the first stage of this development have been found at Giggleswick in Yorkshire and at Danzig in Germany.

Dug-outs are the most widespread of all primitive types of boat. They are still found almost all over the world and have been in use since long before the dawn of history. A Chinese drawing of about a hundred years ago (Fig. 27) may serve to give some sort of an idea of what the Brigg boat may have looked like when afloat. It is interesting for its own sake too. The drum and the gong, the man beating time with a fan, the little idol in a box, the steersman with his large paddle, and the decorations of bow and stern are all worth attention.

Quite near the Brigg boat, though on the other side

Fig. 27. DUG-OUT
From a Chinese drawing of about 1825

of the present course of the river Ancholme, there was found an extraordinary raft, 40 feet long and 9 feet wide in the middle. It was built up of five planks, each running the whole length, shaped so that the width was reduced to $5\frac{1}{2}$ feet at one end and $6\frac{1}{2}$ at the other. On each plank there were ten 'handles' just like those on the patch in the dug-out. Cross-bars were stuck through the rows of handles and wedged tight, while the joints between the planks were not only caulked with moss, but were covered with thin strips of wood lashed in place by thongs passing through rows of holes along the edges of the planks. The date of this raft is uncertain; it may perhaps belong properly to the next chapter, but it is mentioned here because it was found so close to the better-known dug-out.

The skin boat was in use in the southern parts of

England before the arrival of the Romans. This we know not from remains, but from Latin authors. Such craft on a very small scale are still found in Wales, where bowl-shaped coracles to carry one man only are used for river-fishing. Canvas is used instead of skins for a covering to the framework of wickerwork or of bent laths (Fig. 28), but other-

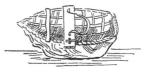

Fig. 28. WELSH CORACLE

wise these coracles are probably very much the same as they were two thousand or more years ago. In Ireland a similar vessel called a ' curragh ' is larger and more boat-shaped.

Still, the craft of which the Romans wrote must have been bigger and more seaworthy than either of these, since there was certainly some cross-Channel traffic. Besides, when Cæsar wanted to cross a river in Spain he set his soldiers to build boats " like those used by the Britons," and he describes them as having keels and ribs of light timber, the rest of the hull being woven out of osier and covered with skins. These must have been bigger than coracles, for it would have been absurd to transport an army in one-man craft. We know that the Britons were such good basket-workers that the Romans took them back to Rome to teach the art there. If one of them could build a boat to carry himself it

Fig. 29. ESKIMO KAYAK

is reasonable to suppose that, within limits, several of them might build a vessel to carry them all.

After all this is exactly what is done by the Eskimo,

who were until quite lately in much the same state of civilization as the early Britons. Their boats are

Fig. 30. Eskimo Umiak
From a model

made of skin stretched over a frame of whalebone, or of wood when it is to be had, and they are of two kinds: the 'kayak' (Fig. 29), used by a single man for hunting and fishing, and the 'umiak' (Fig. 30), a much bigger

Fig. 31. Irish Wicker Vessel
About 1670

vessel used to carry a whole family or more. There can be little doubt that the ancient Britons had craft that were quite as seaworthy as these.

Something of the sort is found in a drawing made about 1670 of a "portable vessel of wicker ordinarily

used by the Wild Irish.'' This drawing, from the Pepys-
ian Library at Cambridge, shows not only the boat
under sail, but also a view of her under construction,
and makes it clear that she was something very like
the boats built by Cæsar's soldiers, with light wooden
keel and ribs and with sides of wicker-
work covered with skins. The whole
appearance of this boat (Fig. 31) is
primitive, but seaworthy. The mast,
with a natural fork used as a lead for
the halliards and with leaves left on
it for ornament, the ox-head on the
stem, and the stone and wood anchor
hanging on the side are all things that
must have looked strange to more
civilized eyes even in the seventeenth
century. Stone anchors of this sort

Fig. 32. MODERN KIL-
LICK, OR STONE ANCHOR

were used countless centuries ago and are still found in
some places. The specimen drawn in Fig. 32 was in use
quite recently at Cape Cod in America.

It seems probable that the Britons had real wooden
planked ships as well. At any rate we know that such
vessels were used by the Veneti, a people living in the
south of Brittany just west of the mouth of the Loire.
Cæsar fought a naval battle against them in the year
56 B.C., and his description of their ships shows that
they were far more advanced than would be expected :

> Their ships were built and rigged in this manner. The
> hulls were somewhat flatter than those of our ships, so that
> they were more suitable for the shallows and the ebbing of
> the tide. The bows were rather upright and they and the
> sterns were suited to the great size of the stormy seas. The
> ships were built entirely of oak, so as to stand any shock.

The cross-timbers were made of beams a foot deep fastened by iron nails an inch thick. The anchors were fitted with iron chains instead of ropes. The sails were of skins and thin leather, either for lack of flax and ignorance of its use or (as is more likely) because sails [of canvas] were not considered able to support such force of wind and drive such heavy ships.

Cæsar must have been used to seeing ships very nearly as advanced as the Roman merchantmen in Figs. 21 and 22, and yet these ships of Brittany seem to have impressed him. There were ships from the west of England in the same fleet, and it seems fair to suppose that they were not so very different ; if they had been wicker vessels surely Cæsar would have mentioned the two distinct types. The chain cables are particularly interesting because such things died out entirely and were not revived until the nineteenth century.

Now the territory of the Veneti was one of the places where the Phœnicians used to come for tin, and Cornwall was another. There must have been plenty of opportunities for both Veneti and Britons to examine Phœnician ships, and after once grasping the principles of strong wooden shipbuilding they would go on building in the same way after the Phœnicians had disappeared. It is worth mentioning that Cornish legend says that St Ia floated over from Ireland on a leaf, and this is just how people accustomed to big, solidly built wooden ships might be expected to describe a coracle built of green wood.

After the actual remains of dug-outs in England and Germany, or even after the descriptions of British coracles and Venetan ships, the representations of Scandinavian vessels that were carved on rocks in

EARLY NORTHERN SHIPS

Norway and Sweden at some time in the last thousand years B.C. are very disappointing. In fact, if it were not for the extraordinary number of these carvings, all very much alike, they might be dismissed as the work of some one who had no idea what he was drawing.

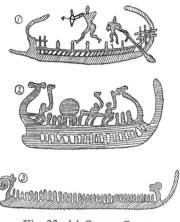

Fig. 33. (1) GREEK GALLEY
(2), (3) SCANDINAVIAN ROCK-CARVINGS

Most of them are far more like sledges than any form of ship which we can imagine, and the fact that there are often dogs in the pictures and never fish rather helps to support the sledge idea. Still they are always found near the coast, and it must be admitted that they are generally accepted as ships. Besides, men are shown fighting in them, and this is certainly more suitable for ships than for sledges. The end that is usually supposed to be the bow is not unlike the double bow of some Central African canoes, but the other end, as a stern, is unique. It is, in fact, so like a ram bow that it is difficult to look on it as anything else. Compare these rock-carvings (Fig. 33) and the similar ships on Danish bronze knives (Fig. 34) with the ships on early Greek vases and the likeness is startling. Whether it was a real ram bow or merely one shaped to imitate a ram depends on how these vessels were built, and of this we know nothing for certain. Probably they were built-

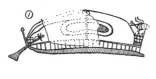

Fig. 34. (1) GREEK GALLEY; (2) SHIP ON DANISH BRONZE KNIFE

up boats of some kind rather than dug-outs. The more complicated carvings seem to show some sort of framework, and some of the Danish vessels look as if they were planked, but all this is very doubtful. It has been suggested that they were built of birch-bark, like the North American canoes. In that case the shape of the bow must have been more a matter of imitation than of design for warlike purposes.

A Swedish writer has recently suggested that these carvings are meant for 'outrigger canoes,' which are dug-outs made less apt to capsize by having on one side a long log of wood joined to the main hull by two or more cross-pieces called 'booms.' Such canoes are very common in the Pacific and the East Indies, but so far there is no other evidence that they were ever used in Europe. Still, it must be admitted that models of such outrigger canoes as drawn by children have produced designs wonderfully like those on the rock-carvings.

On the whole it seems probable that some of the peoples on the shores of the North Sea must have had real planked ships long before the Roman conquest of Britain. Apparently there was intercourse between Scotland and Norway, and such intercourse could never have been carried on in either dug-outs or bark canoes.

EARLY NORTHERN SHIPS

It must be admitted that our evidence for this intercourse depends on a rather doubtful source : the supposed travels of Pytheas in the North, and the identification of his " Thule " with Norway. Pytheas, whose accounts of his voyages we know only from quotations by later writers, was a Greek astronomer from Marseilles. He sailed from the Mediterranean to England somewhere about 300 B.C., and from the northernmost point of Scotland went on to an inhabited land called Thule, where the longest day was as long as twenty-one or twenty-two hours, and where he heard tales of the midnight sun still farther to the north. It is difficult to find any country save Norway that will fit the description, and it seems clear that Pytheas went there deliberately and not by accident. Thus the way must have been known, and either Norse or Scottish vessels must have crossed the North Sea many times before.

The peoples of Northern Europe may have been barbarians in some ways before they came in contact with the civilization of Rome, but if they could build ships fit to cross the North Sea and fit to meet those of Rome in battle they cannot have been so far behind in the matter of shipbuilding and seamanship.

CHAPTER IV

THE DAYS OF THE DOUBLE-ENDED SHIP
A.D. 200–1200

EVEN if we had no evidence at all that any of the Northern nations had made much progress in the art of shipbuilding before the Roman invasion of Britain we should be obliged to assume that such was the case because of the very high level that is reached by an example of Northern shipbuilding of the third century A.D. This vessel, found in 1863 at Nydam in Schleswig—once Danish, then German, now Danish again—is not only such a fine piece of work that she must be the product of centuries of experience, but is also so different from any Roman ship that her builders must have been working on an entirely separate line of development.

Roman ships, as far as our knowledge goes, were always carvel-built, with their planks fitted edge to edge so as to make a smooth surface. The Nydam boat (Fig. 35), like all other surviving examples of Northern shipping of the first ten centuries A.D., is clinker-built, with the lower edge of each plank overlapping the upper edge of the plank beneath it. There is another very striking difference, in the shape of the hull. In Roman ships the bow and the stern were quite unlike one another ; in Northern ships of this period the two ends are almost exactly the same. This double-ended hull is mentioned by Tacitus in about A.D. 100 as a char-

66

acteristic of the ships of the Suiones or Scandinavians, and the Nydam boat, now preserved at Kiel, is a perfect illustration of the type.

She is about 76 feet long over all and 11 feet wide; amidships she is just over 4 feet deep, while the extreme points of her stem and sternpost rise 10 feet above the line of her keel. As a matter of fact she has no real keel

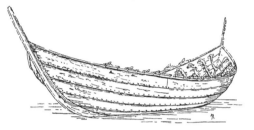

Fig. 35. THE NYDAM BOAT

in the modern sense, but has only a centre-line plank, thicker and wider than the others, 3 inches thick and 2 feet wide amidships, but tapering off at the ends to about 8 inches wide where it joins the stem and stern-post and at the same time increasing in depth to 6 inches. On each side of this keel-plank there are five planks, the uppermost shaped so that its top edge forms a gunwale about 6 inches thick. The planks were joined to one another and to the stem and sternpost by means of iron nails riveted on the inside over washers, or 'rooves,' exactly as is done to-day. The ribs—nineteen in number—were not nailed to the planks as is done nowadays, but were lashed to projecting 'clamps' left on the inside of the planks in the same way as those on the patch in the Brigg boat. The construction of this boat and of some others belonging to this period will be seen in Fig. 41.

Evidently the planking must have been put together first, and the ribs, cut from naturally curved timber, must have been added afterward. The rowlocks for fourteen oars on each side are cut from single pieces of wood (Fig. 36) and are lashed to the gunwale in such a way that it would be possible to reverse them and to row the boat the other way round.

Fig. 36. ROWLOCK OF NYDAM BOAT

Simple 'backing water' for a short time was provided for by having the oars held to the rowlocks by lashings passing through the holes. The 'thwarts,' or seats for the rowers, rested on the clamps of the gunwale-plank and fitted over the ends of the ribs; they were supported by uprights resting on the ribs beneath them. The rudder (Fig. 37) was shaped like a wide-bladed oar or paddle. It is not quite clear how it was fitted, but the curiously shaped handle at the top was evidently a primitive form of tiller by which it was turned. There was no trace of mast or sail or of any means of supporting a mast; this agrees with the statement of Tacitus that the Suiones did not use sails.

Fig. 37

RUDDER OF NYDAM BOAT

There were some remarkable facts about the discovery of this boat. First, holes had been cut in her planking with the obvious purpose of sinking her. Secondly, she was heavily loaded with gear, and some of this seems to have been thrown overboard. Thirdly, parts of two other boats were found near, and one of them seems to have had something in the nature of a ram at each end. Perhaps the Nydam boat was returning from some plundering expedition, and her

68

crew, finding themselves pursued, preferred to throw away their booty and sink their boat rather than leave them for their enemies. The coins found in and near the boat date from between A.D. 69 and 217, so her date is probably somewhere about the middle or end of the third century.

For our next examples of early ships we have to turn to Norway and to skip some six hundred years. This brings us to the days of the Vikings, who were so essentially a seafaring people that their chiefs were even buried in their own private boats. Burial in great mounds is a very ancient and a very widespread custom; the Pyramids are an exaggerated example of this. In the North burial-mounds are usually simpler structures with perhaps a few stones to mark the entrance. There are, however, many cases in Sweden and in the countries to the south and east of the Baltic where the grave consists of stones carefully arranged to represent a boat, and there are other cases, particularly in Norway, where actual boats have been used as burial-chambers and have then been covered by mounds of earth.

It is to this custom that we owe most of our knowledge of the appearance and the construction of ships of about the ninth century. Many of the Norwegian mounds have been explored, and in several cases they have yielded recognizable fragments of boats. Better still, two of the mounds were found to contain boats well enough preserved to allow of almost complete restoration.

At Gunnarshaug in the island of Karmö, near Stavanger, the remains of a boat were unearthed in 1887. It was in very bad condition, but it was possible to make out that it had been a clinker-built vessel about 16 feet wide with a keel about 65 feet long. In its arrangements for rowing it differed from the Nydam boat, since its oars had worked through round holes in a plank fitted above the two heavy strips of timber (Fig. 41) which corresponded to the gunwale of the Nydam boat. There was nothing to show that this boat had been intended for sailing, but in the three best preserved of these Norwegian boats, those from Tune, Gokstad, and Oseberg, there is no doubt on the matter, because in them the arrangements for supporting the mast are perfectly clear. These three finds all belong to the south-eastern part of the country, and may well represent a different type from the Gunnarshaug boat.

The Tune boat, from near Sarpsborg on the Glommen river, east of Oslo Fjord, need not be discussed at any great length because everything found in it is shown better in the more perfect boats from Gokstad and Oseberg. It was found in 1867 and was clinker-built, about 45 feet long on the keel and about 14 feet wide. The two ends and the upper planks had disappeared, but the elaborate 'step' for the mast was well preserved.

The Oseberg boat (Fig. 38) was discovered in 1903 about three miles above the present mouth of a small river which runs into the sea just west of the entrance to Oslo Fjord. It had been used as the burial-chamber of a woman, no doubt the wife of some great chief. After being dug out it was carefully put together again and is now exhibited in Oslo. This vessel is 70 feet 6 inches long from stem to sternpost and 16 feet 9 inches wide amidships. Her keel is 65 feet long, and her depth amidships, from the lower side of the keel to the upper edge of the top plank, is 5 feet 3 inches. She has a real keel like that of a modern boat, 10 inches deep and

PLATE II

MODEL OF A ROMAN SHIP (A.D. 50)
Made by Dr Jules Sottas

PLATE III

SHIP ON THE FONT IN WINCHESTER CATHEDRAL (1180)
The earliest known representation of a stern-rudder

8 inches wide at the top. On each side of this keel there are twelve planks ; the tenth, counting from the keel, is much thicker than the others and is really a strip of timber cut into an **L**-shaped section (Fig. 41). The ribs come up as far as this tenth plank, and are bolted to it and to the next plank beneath it. They are lashed to the rest of the bottom planks by means of clamps of a rather more elaborate pattern than those of the Nydam

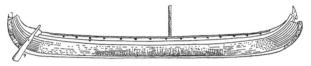

Fig. 38. THE OSEBERG SHIP

boat, but they are not attached to the keel in any way. The planking is fixed together and to the keel with iron nails or rivets. From end to end of each rib runs a beam, and above each beam there is a pair of ' knees,' which supports the two uppermost rows of planking. The top plank has round holes for the oars, fifteen in number and about 3 feet 4 inches apart.

The mast is stepped nearly 3 feet before the middle of the ship. Its foot rested in a hole in a large block of wood which lay on the keel and was slotted out to fit over two of the ribs. This block was not fixed down in any way ; it was held in position simply by the slots and by two strips of wood nailed to the ribs on each side of it. About 3 feet higher up the mast was held between the two legs of a long piece of wood something like a clothes-peg. This was fixed to four of the beams ; it was curved upward in the middle, and the beam just before the mast was also curved. The mast was thus supported from forward and from the sides, but was free to fall aft. To prevent it from doing this at the wrong moment it was held firm by a third piece of wood which fitted between its after side and a step cut across the two legs of the main support.

The rudder was something like that of the Nydam boat in shape, but its blade was longer and straighter. It was carried on the right-hand side, as was always the case in Northern ships with a single side-rudder. This is why the right-hand side of a ship is called the starboard side. 'Starboard' is simply a very slightly changed form of 'steer-board,' the steering-side. The rudder was held to the ship's side in two places : by a strap of plaited leather near the upper edge of the planking and by a long strip of flexible root of a fir-tree, passing through a hole in the rudder-blade, through a large rounded block of oak projecting about 16 inches from the ship's side, through the seventh plank from the keel, and finally through a heavy timber which extended from the keel to the gunwale. In the top of the rudder-head was a slot cut at right angles to the blade so that the tiller lay across the ship instead of fore and aft as is usual nowadays. The helmsman sat between the tiller and the stern and pushed the tiller away from him to turn to port or pulled it toward him to turn to starboard.

There was no real deck, but there were floor-boards fitted between the beams. Right at the ends of the boat the floor-boards were raised a few inches to form two separate platforms. No seats for the rowers were found, but they must have rowed sitting because the oar-ports are not much more than a foot above the floor-boards.

All sorts of things were found in the ship. There were sledges, a wagon, bedsteads, chests, buckets, bones of horses and oxen, and many other objects. Everything possible was decorated with wonderful carving. This is not only the case with the things in the ship, but even with the stem and sternpost of the ship herself (Fig. 39). All this carving has been a means of dating the find

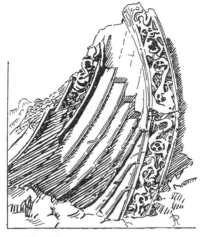

Fig. 39. BOW OF OSEBERG SHIP

very exactly, and experts have concluded that the burial took place between 835 and 850 and that the ship herself was probably a few years older.

Until the discovery of the Oseberg ship the best example of a Viking ship had been the vessel found in 1880 at Gokstad near Sandefjord, only about fourteen miles south of Oseberg. This ship is also preserved in Oslo (Fig. 40), and fortunately she was in such good condition that it was possible to transport her in two complete portions which were easily joined up again. She is believed to date from about 900, and it will be seen that there are points about her which certainly seem to suggest a later date than that of the Oseberg ship.

The two vessels are not very different in size, though

the Gokstad ship belongs to a rather more seaworthy type. Her keel is 66 feet long, and she is 78 feet long over all. The explanation of the much greater 'rake,' or overhang, at the ends is that the stem and sternpost are not fixed directly to the keel, as in the Oseberg ship, but are attached to other pieces which are in turn fixed to the ends of the keel. In breadth the two ships are

Fig. 40. THE GOKSTAD SHIP

the same, 16 feet 9 inches, but in depth the Gokstad ship with her 6 feet 9 inches is as much as 18 inches the larger. She has sixteen planks a side, as compared with twelve. The beams rest on the frames at the tenth plank and have knees above them for the upper planks just as in the Oseberg ship, but this tenth plank is no longer cut in a special shape ; it is simply a rather thicker plank than the rest and the curve of the side is quite continuous, instead of being broken at this point. This difference is shown in Fig. 41.

Naturally, with six upper planks instead of two the side above the beams is very much higher. It is, therefore, quite natural to find that the oar-ports are cut in the third plank from the top instead of the uppermost. Even so, they are much higher above the beams than in the Oseberg ship. The oar-ports are just about

74

the same distance apart, but there are sixteen of them on each side and they are fitted on the inside with small shutters to close them when the oars were not in use. One interesting feature about this Gokstad ship was

the remains of a row of shields fixed all along the side, covering the oar-ports (Fig. 42). This may have been their position in harbour and perhaps when sailing, but obviously they would have to be moved for rowing, and they can hardly have been very secure when the ship was under sail.

In a general way the two boats are very much alike. Such differences as there are can easily be explained by the natural improvement in ship-building and by the fact that the Oseberg ship belonged to a woman, while the Gokstad ship belonged to a man, and, in fact, to a very big and very strong man, as can be told from the bones that were found in her.

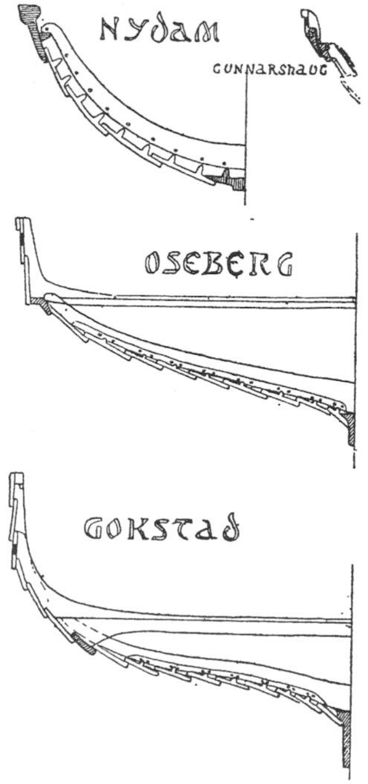

Fig. 41
MIDSHIP SECTIONS OF DANISH
AND NORWEGIAN VESSELS

As in the case of the Oseberg ship, all sorts of things had been buried in the ship, among them being no less than twelve horses and six dogs. Many of the wooden and metal objects are decorated, though not to such an extent as in the later find. There were, though, in this ship, besides all the usual household articles, fragments of three smaller boats. They were not in a condition

75

to allow of restoration, but it can be said that their construction was similar to that of the ship herself and that at any rate two of them had been fitted for sailing. Their rowlocks were like those of the Nydam boat, but were nailed to the gunwale. The keel of the largest was more than 25 feet long, and that of the smallest was $13\frac{1}{2}$ feet.

The roof seen in the drawing (Fig. 40) was not a part of the ship, but was added to cover the body of the dead

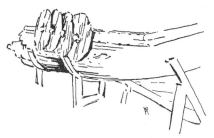

chief. There were, however, carved supports for spreading an awning of much the same shape. There is no doubt as to the seaworthiness of this Gokstad ship, because a full-sized copy of her was made and sailed across the Atlantic for the

Fig. 42. SHIELDS ON THE SIDE OF THE GOKSTAD SHIP

Chicago Exhibition of 1892. She is said to have made a speed as high as ten knots at times on the way.

In the north of Germany there have been found remains of boats of very much the same shape as these Scandinavian vessels, but of rather different construction. In length of keel they range from 29 feet to 50 feet. The longest, with a keel 5 feet longer than the keel-plank of the Nydam boat, seems to have been about 2 feet narrower, but the others are more normal in their proportions. The remarkable thing about them is that they all have ribs cut in steps to fit the planking and fastened firmly to it with wooden pins, or 'trenails.' This rather suggests a later date, but the whole matter is very uncertain. A much bigger vessel found at Broesen near Danzig in 1874 belonged almost certainly to the fifteenth century, if not later.

One other find must be mentioned. This is a boat dug up in 1899 near Bruges in Belgium. She belonged to a very different type, for she was absolutely flat-bottomed. She had no keel, and her stem and sternpost rose at a sharp angle from the flat bottom which was as much as 6 feet wide amidships. Above it there were seven planks on each side. Her total length was 47½ feet, and her greatest breadth 11½ feet. The mast which was stepped in one of the cross-timbers on the bottom was 33 feet long, and there were still traces of a woollen sail left on the yard. The rudder was almost exactly like that of the Nydam boat.

Here again the date is not very certain, but the boat belongs in all probability to somewhere near the Viking period. The flat bottom was a necessary consequence of local conditions and has always been a characteristic of the ships of the Netherlands. We shall see shortly that in the time of King Alfred English shipbuilders recognized two distinct foreign types : the Frisian and the Danish. It may well be that in this Belgian boat and in those from Norway we have small examples of these two types.

Certainly the Viking ships that have been preserved are not specimens of the real warship. They are vessels of fifteen or sixteen pairs of oars, whereas big warships had usually from twenty to thirty and sometimes more. The *Long Serpent* of A.D. 1000 had thirty-four pairs of oars, and Canute's largest ship a few years later is said to have had as many as sixty. The Norse Sagas, which are writings combining history and legend, give a certain amount of information about ships, but hardly ever stoop to dimensions. Still they do frequently mention the number of pairs of oars, and from this we can get a fairly good idea of the length of the ships. On the proportions of the Oseberg ship the length of Canute's big vessel would be about 297 feet, and on those of the Gokstad ship about 307. Her actual length is said to have been 300 feet. This seems very long, but it is difficult to see how she could have been much less. The distance between oars could not be reduced, and anything of the bireme type was unknown in the North, except for three ships built in Norway in 1206.

Alfred the Great built big ships in England when he was fighting the Danes. He has often been called " the Father of the English Navy." This does not mean that he was the first king to own warships, but rather that he was the first to use his ships properly by meeting the enemy at sea and trying to prevent them from landing. No doubt Alfred's ships were more or less similar to the normal double-ended Viking type, but they were bigger than previous English ships and had improvements of the King's own devising. The chronicles tell us that " they were full twice as long as the others ; some had sixty oars and some had more ; they were both swifter and steadier and also higher than the others ; they were shaped neither like the Frisian nor the Danish, but so as it seemed to him they would be most efficient."

Near Botley on the Hamble river, which flows into Southampton Water, there are the remains of an ancient ship of some sort. Her figurehead, which was a lion, is said to have been removed about a hundred years ago, and a good deal of her timber was cut up in 1875. A small part of her planking is preserved in the West Gate at Winchester. Her keel is said to have been as much as 130 feet long, and if she belongs to the Saxon and Danish period at all—which is very doubtful—she must have been a ship of at least thirty pairs of oars.

As far as one can tell there must have been very little change in Northern ships between 900 and 1100. The

Fig. 43. ENGLISH SHIP, FROM THE BAYEUX TAPESTRY

ships of Harold and of William the Conqueror seem to have been simply enlarged copies of the Gokstad ship. Unfortunately, we know them only from a rather unsatisfactory source—the Bayeux Tapestry, made at least fifty years after the Norman invasion by ladies who possibly had never seen a ship at all, and who had only the ordinary materials of needlework at their disposal. Still, the ships look as if they have been based on drawings or directions by some one who did understand what he was doing. There is an interesting difference between the English and Norman ships that would hardly have been thought of except by some one who really knew the two types. All Harold's ships, with one exception, have a break in the line of the side amidships. Fig. 43 shows this break quite clearly just abreast of the mast with oar-ports in the top plank before and abaft it. Nothing of the sort appears in the Norman ships (Fig. 44). One of William's ships is shown unshipping her mast before being pulled up on the beach, and apparently the figureheads were also removed when the ships were out of the water. At least one ship seems to have shrouds to her mast. This is an important point, because it suggests that by then it must have

Fig. 44. NORMAN SHIPS, FROM THE BAYEUX TAPESTRY

been the practice to make use of a beam wind at least. As long as the mast was given only a stay and a backstay it is probable that ships sailed only with the wind more or less behind them ; as soon as they tried to use a beam wind, or one at right angles to their course, it would be necessary to give the mast more sideways support, and shrouds would be introduced to do this. It may be that the earlier Norwegian ships had shrouds, but there is no sign of them or of fastenings for them in either the Oseberg or the Gokstad ship.

There is another representation of a ship of the same general type on the seal of La Rochelle in France (Fig. 45). Nearly all seaport towns have at some time used a seal with a ship on it, and these seals have been preserved on documents. The difficulty is that the date of a document does not necessarily date the seal which it carries, still less the ship on that seal. The same seal has often been used for centuries; for instance, Southampton still uses a seal made in 1587, and the ship given there would be a poor example of a modern man-of-war. Still, by taking the earliest date which can be derived from a document, and by comparing the style of workmanship of one seal with another, it is possible to get a fairly good idea of the date of most of these ship seals. That of La Rochelle is believed to belong to the twelfth century, so it can hardly be more than a hundred years later than the Bayeux Tapestry and is quite possibly contemporary. It shows exactly the same double-ended one-masted ship with clinker-built hull and with

Fig. 45. SEAL OF LA ROCHELLE
Twelfth century

high stem and sternpost. Besides this it shows a very important feature about the sail. The vertical lines on the lower part of the sail are almost certainly 'reef-points,' by which part of the sail could be tied up in a bundle at the foot when it was necessary to shorten sail. Ships of the Middle Ages had two ways of varying their sail-area. Sometimes they used reef-points, and sometimes they added or removed a piece of canvas called the 'bonnet' at the bottom of the sail. This second method seems to have been the more usual, and representations of reef-points are quite rare before the middle of the seventeenth century. They do, however, occur quite often enough for us to be sure that reefs were in use at any rate between 1200 and 1500. After that we know little or nothing of them

81

before 1650, or thereabouts, but from then onward they have been in universal use right up to the present day.

The next two seals, and others of the same kind and period, show the final appearance of the double-ended ship at a date when she was already being superseded by an improved design. The two illustrated are the thirteenth-century seals of Sandwich and Winchelsea. Together they give a number of most interesting details. Sandwich (Fig. 46) shows 'castles' built, or rather fitted, at each end and a 'topcastle' on the mast. We can see the ship's boat carried on deck amidships and a hook for cutting an enemy's rigging. There are two prongs sticking out from the sternpost; more often these are shown in one piece on top of the sternpost, and in that form this fitting, called the 'mike,' is quite a characteristic of thirteenth-century ships. It seems to have been used for all sorts of odd jobs. Often the backstay is fastened to it, sometimes it carries a coil of rope, and in one picture it supports rope, anchor, and spears. From its shape one would guess that it was meant originally for supporting the mast when lowered. Egyptian ships had something very similar, and modern sailing-boats have a like fitting for carrying the boom. The three lumps on the side are no doubt 'fender cleats' to protect the planking from damage against a quay. One most important fitting appears here for almost the first time. This is the bowsprit projecting

Fig. 46. SEAL OF SANDWICH
Thirteenth century

over the bow. This spar will be considered in the next chapter. The Winchelsea ship (Fig. 47) has no bowsprit and no topcastle, but its ' forecastle ' and ' aftercastle ' are more highly developed. As it gives the starboard side of the ship it shows the whole of the side-rudder, which only just appears in the other example. It shows also an interesting detail in the way the anchor is being raised, with two men working on a windlass abaft the mast and two others hauling directly on the cable.

It is worth considering why Northern ships should suddenly have acquired so many new fittings about 1200 after having remained very much the same for several centuries.

Fig. 47. SEAL OF WINCHELSEA
Thirteenth century

The most likely explanation is the increase of intercourse with the Mediterranean, caused to some extent by the establishment of the Normans in Italy and Sicily as well as in the North and more definitely by the Crusades. In the Third Crusade, which began in 1188, ships from the ports on both sides of the English Channel entered the Mediterranean as a fleet for the first time in history. As builders of seaworthy ships the Northerners may have had little to fear in a comparison with the peoples of the Mediterranean, but in matters of accommodation and of labour-saving devices the latter, with an older civilization behind them, would be likely to lead the way, and it is just in this sort of thing that Northern ships seem to have

83

developed at the end of the twelfth and the beginning of the thirteenth centuries.

A few years later the Northern ship with improvements of her own returned to establish herself in the Mediterranean, and there she received the final touches that led, in the course of the fifteenth century, to the adoption throughout Europe of one standard type, the full-rigged ship.

CHAPTER V

THE ONE-MASTED SHIP IN HER PRIME
A.D. 1200–1400

IF a typical ship of the twelfth century could be put beside one of the fourteenth the difference in rig would be very small indeed. In each case there would be a single mast with a square sail rather high and narrow to modern ideas. A bowsprit might be found in the one and not in the other, but otherwise there would be very little difference. The important change would be in the hull alone.

Northern ships of Viking and Norman times were, as we have seen, double-ended—that is to say, there was little or no difference in the shape of their bow and stern. As long as ships were steered by oars or by oar-shaped rudders hung over one side near the stern there was no reason to alter this double-ended design. Directly the idea of a rudder on the actual sternpost was thought of it became desirable to alter the shape of the sternpost to suit it. It was not impossible to hang a rudder on a curved sternpost—in fact this was done for many years in Mediterranean galleys—but a straight sternpost would be so much more convenient that it followed almost as a matter of course. Hanging a rudder on to the sternpost is very much like hanging a door on to its post, and it is obvious how much simpler this is if the two edges are straight. With the introduction of the straight sternpost the two ends of the ship were bound to differ in shape, unless the stem were made straight as well. This never happened in big ships, though the stem did become rather more upright than in the old type of ship.

The date and the place of the invention of the stern-rudder are not yet definitely established. As far as one

Fig. 48. STERN OF A DUTCH BOAT
About 1660

can judge at present, it came in toward the end of the twelfth century, and probably first became general in Germany and the Netherlands. The earliest-known example of a ship with a stern-rudder is on the font in Winchester Cathedral, and is shown in Plate III. This is believed to be Belgian work of about 1180. It is only right to mention that some people question the date, and that others deny that it is a stern-rudder at all. In this latter dispute the point is really whether the beast's head is on the top of the sternpost or is a decoration to the rudder itself, such as is often found in later vessels (Fig. 48). If it is on the sternpost it certainly seems that the rudder must be on one side, and is, therefore, only a very highly developed kind of side-rudder. This idea seems to be contradicted by the run of the planks toward the stern. The three lines of decoration run up at the bow into the beast's head, but at the stern they miss the head altogether and suggest that it is on the rudder, and is not part of the actual ship at all.

Apart from this font and another somewhat similar in Belgium, the first dated stern-rudder is on the seal of Elbing in Germany (Fig. 49). This has been traced as far back as 1242, and Wismar, another German town, has a seal of 1256 which also shows the modern rudder. In England the first examples are the seal of Poole (1325), and the coins called 'gold nobles' issued by Edward III in 1344 to commemorate his victory

Fig. 49. SEAL OF ELBING
Thirteenth century

Fig. 50. ENGLISH GOLD NOBLE,
1344

at Sluys (Fig. 50). The seal of Ipswich (Fig. 51) is perhaps earlier and may be nearly as old as the Winchester font, but it has not yet been found on any document of earlier date than 1349.

Nowadays the position of a ship's rudder is so much a matter of course that we hardly give it a thought. In spite of this, the invention of the stern-rudder must be looked on as one of the most important steps in the history of the ship. It was one of the three things that transformed the Viking boat into the real sailing-ship, able to take full advantage of any wind. The others were a deep-draught hull and a bowsprit. We say "were" because in more recent years different rigs and such things as 'centre-boards' have rather altered the position. A hull that goes down a long way under

87

water is far better for sailing close to the wind than one of shallow draught. This was discovered probably by the trader, who built his ship with an eye to cargo-carrying and found that though she was slower than the long ship she had more possibilities under sail.

To take full advantage of a more ' weatherly ' hull the sail had to be made to set better. When the ship

Fig. 51. SEAL OF IPSWICH
Thirteenth century

was ' close-hauled,' or as near the wind as she would go, the ' luff,' or forward edge of the sail, would flap and try to curl away from the wind. To cure this, ropes called ' bowlines ' were fixed to the luff and led forward. In a short ship with a big sail it was necessary to take the bowlines farther forward even than the stem, and for this the bowsprit was used.

Bowlines are not definitely shown on any of the seals drawn here, but it is very likely that the two slack lines under the bowsprit in the Sandwich ship are really a bowline disconnected from its sail. The seal of San Sebastian in Spain, with a ship of just the same type, shows a bowline attached to the sail and leading to the bowsprit in exactly the same way.

When once sailing to windward, or trying to, was a possibility, the side-rudder would soon prove unsatisfactory. With the wind on the starboard side and the ship heeling over to port, the rudder would be nearly out of the water. In the Mediterranean there was a rudder on each side, and the difficulty was not quite so great, but in the North the second side-rudder never became usual, and the central stern-rudder was the only other way out of it. It was really a far better way, as can be proved from the fact that the stern-rudder was not very long in displacing the two side-rudders in the Mediterranean as well.

Possibly the two kinds of rudder, and the two designs of hull that they caused, may have been the distinguishing marks of the two mediæval types, the ' nef ' and the ' cog.' Both these names are found in the thirteenth and fourteenth centuries for big ships, and there was undoubtedly some clear distinction between them since a document of 1226 describes a fleet as consisting of six cogs and seven nefs. If so the cog was probably the new type with the stern-rudder.

As early as 1252 we find the Port Books of Damme and Bruges in Flanders distinguishing between ships " with a rudder on the side " and those " with a rudder astern." The latter paid the bigger dues, so were probably the larger. Other Flemish, Dutch, and German documents of the thirteenth century give four different kinds of steering apparatus : ' kuelroeder,' ' hangroeder,' ' sleeproeder,' and ' hantroeder.' Ships with the first of these paid the largest dues ; those with the hantroeder paid least. Usually the hangroeder paid more than the sleeproeder, but occasionally it was the other way round.

The hangroeder, or hinged rudder (*pendulum gubernaculum* in the Latin documents), seems to have been the ordinary stern-rudder such as we see on small boats to-day. The hantroeder, or hand rudder (*manuale* in Latin), must have been a steering-oar. The sleep-roeder is sometimes explained as 'rudder on the side,' and was thus the ordinary side-rudder of the twelfth century. What exactly the kuelroeder was is a harder question. One German document translates it as *Lochsteuer*, and both words mean in English 'hole-rudder.' Probably this means that either the rudder-head or the tiller passed through a hole in the hull. This would be necessary in the case of ships with sterncastles at all solidly built, and such ships would naturally be the biggest. It is tempting to suggest that it might mean a rudder working in a slot, or ' trunk,' like those of Chinese craft, but this is perhaps too far-fetched an idea.

It will be noticed that the ship on the seal of Elbing has no sail and not even a yard visible. The same is the case with Dutch seals which show the same sort of hull. A good example of this is the seal of Harderwijk (Fig. 52), which dates from 1280 or earlier. It has been suggested that these seals show not only a smaller kind of ship, a vessel for coasting or inland use, but even one with a different rig altogether, having a ' spritsail ' and foresail like the modern Thames barge. These other kinds of sails will be discussed in the next chapter, but it may be mentioned here that the earliest-known undoubted spritsail comes from a miniature believed to have been painted about 1416. Certainly the size of the helmsman in the Elbing ship makes her look very small, but true scale was not the strong point of mediæval artists, as the gold noble shows, and it would never be safe to guess at the size of their ships from the size of the men in them. As to the question of rig, there is really not enough detail in any of the seals to settle the question either way.

Very few of the ships on seals show as much life and movement as that drawn in Fig. 53 from the seal of Stralsund (1329). Here we have a fine ship, with an aftercastle that has a far more permanent look than

Fig. 52. SEAL OF HARDERWIJK
Thirteenth century

Fig. 53. SEAL OF STRALSUND
Fourteenth century

those on older seals and that illustrates the possible meaning of a ' hole-rudder ' very well. She is sailing before the wind in quite a rough sea. As usual, the man is far too big for the ship, and the artist has also gone astray over the perspective of the shrouds, but otherwise the ship is wonderfully well proportioned and lifelike.

For an idea of what a sea-voyage was like in one of these ships one cannot do better than to turn to a poem which has been preserved in a manuscript at Trinity College, Cambridge. The actual manuscript belongs to the fifteenth century, but the poem seems likely to be rather earlier ; certainly the ship seems to have had only one mast and thus to be more typical of the century before.

THE SAILING-SHIP

Men may leve all gamys
That saylen to Seynt Jamys
For many a man hit gramys
    When they begyn to sayle.
For when that they have take the see
At Sandwyche or at Wynchelsee
At Bristow or where that hit be
    Theyr herts begyn to fayle.

Anone the mastyr commandeth fast
To hys shypmen in all the hast
To dresse hem sone about the mast
    Theyr takeling to make.
With howe hissa then they cry
What howe mate thou stondyst to ny
Thy fellow may nat hale the by
    Thus they begyn to crake.

A boy or tweyn anone up styen
And overtwhart the sayleyerd lyen
Yhow talya the remenaunt cryen
    And pull with all theyr myght.
Bestowe the bote boteswayne anone
That our pylgryms may pley thereon
For som ar lyke to cowgh and grone
    Or hit be ful mydnyght.

Hale the bowelyne now vere the shete
Coke make redy anone our mete
Our pylgryms have no lust to ete
    I pray God geve hem rest.
Go to the helm what howe no nere
Steward felow a pot of bere
Ye shall have ser with good chere
    Anone all of the best.

Yhowe trussa hale in the brayles
Thow halyst nat be god thow fayles
O se howe well owre good shyp sayles
    And thus they say among.

THE ONE-MASTED SHIP

Hale in the wartake hit shalbe done
Steward cover the boorde anone
And set bred and salt thereone
    And tary nat to long.

Then cometh one and seyth be mery
Ye shal have a storme or a pery
Holde thow thy pese thow canst no whery
    Thow medlyst wonder sore.
Thys mene cohyle the pylgryms ly
And have theyr bolys fast theym by
And cry aftyr hote malvesy
    Theyr helthe for to restore.

And som wold have a saltyd tost
For they myght ete neyther sode ne rost
A man myght sone pay for theyr cost
    As for oo day or twayne.
Some layde theyr bookys on theyr kne
And rad so long they myght nat se
Alas myne hede woll cleve on thre
    Thus seyth another certayne.

Then cometh owre owner lyke a lorde
And speketh many a royall worde
And dresseth hym to the hygh borde
    To see all thyngs be well.
Anone he calleth a carpentere
And byddyth hym bryng with hym hys gere
To make the cabans here and there
    With many a febyll cell.

A sak of strawe were there ryght good
For som must lyg theym mi theyr hood
I had as lefe be in the wood
    Without mete or drynk.
For when that we shall go to bedde
The pumpe was nygh our bedde hede
A man were as good to be dede
    As smell therof the stynk.

THE SAILING-SHIP

A 'translation' may help to show up some of the interesting points about this poem :

Men that sail to St James may say farewell to all pleasures, for many people suffer when they set sail. For when they have put to sea from Sandwich or Winchelsea or Bristol, or wherever it happens to be, their hearts begin to fail.

Soon the master orders his seamen to hurry up and take their places round the mast for setting sail. Then they cry " Yo ho, hoist ! What ho, mate, you are standing too close, your comrade has not room to haul." Thus they begin to talk.

A boy or two climb up at once and lie across the yard ; the rest cry " Yo ho, tally ! " and pull with all their might. " Get the boat stowed, boatswain, for our pilgrims to occupy themselves with it, for some of them will very likely be coughing and groaning before it is midnight."

" Haul the bowline. Now veer the sheet. Cook, make our food ready at once. Our pilgrims have no desire to eat. I pray God to give them rest. Go to the helm. What ho ! No closer. Steward fellow, a pot of beer." " You shall have, sir, with good cheer, all of the best directly."

" Yo ho, truss ! Haul in the brails. You are not hauling ; by God, you are shirking. Oh, see how well our good ship sails." And that is how they talk. " Haul in the wartack." " It shall be done." " Steward, lay the table at once and put bread and salt on it, and don't take too long about it."

Then some one comes and says : " Be merry, you will have a storm or a squall." " Be quiet. You never can. You are a sorry meddler." Meanwhile the pilgrims lie with their bowls close beside them and shout for hot Malvoisie wine to restore their health.

And some ask for a salted toast, because they cannot eat either boiled or roast meat. A man could just as well pay for their keep for two days as for one. Some laid their books on their knees and read till they could see no longer. " Alas, my head will split in three," so says another, " I am certain of it."

94

Then our owner comes like a lord and speaks many royal words and goes to the high table to see everything is well. Presently he calls a carpenter and tells him to bring his gear to make cabins here and there and many small compartments.

"A sack of straw would be very good there, for some of them will have to sleep in their cloaks." "I would as soon be in the wood without meat or drink; for when we go to bed the pump will be close to the head of our bed, and a man who smells its stink is as good as dead."

There are a few points about the third, fourth, and fifth verses that want a little explanation. The boys are sent aloft to cut the lashings round the sail as it is hoisted. The word 'tally' means 'haul.' It is a little difficult at first sight to see why they should haul in the bowline and 'veer,' or slack out, the sheet at the same time. In an ordinary way both would be eased off with the wind aft, and both hauled in for sailing close to the wind. Sir Alan Moore suggests what seems a probable explanation. This is that they wanted the whole sail as far forward as possible to make the ship 'pay off,' or turn away from the wind. With several sails this can be done by setting the head-sails first, but with only the one sail it would be necessary to do something of this sort.

Having got going, they seem to have sailed with the wind on one side. The order "no nere" to the helmsman means that he is to be careful not to let the ship come up into the wind too much. Next, after asking for his pot of beer, the master notices that the wind is getting up and decides to shorten sail. He does this by 'trussing up' the sail a bit by means of the brails. The word 'truss' had several meanings. One was simply a 'down-haul' on the yard, another was a tackle which helped to hold the yard to the mast. In connexion with brails its meaning is certainly 'gather up.' Evidently the wind was increasing, for the exclamation about the speed of the ship is followed by the hint from one of the crew that there is 'dirty weather' coming. The 'wartake' was some sort of extra rope for controlling the sail. In an ordinary way the 'tack' controlled the 'clew,' or lower corner of the sail nearest the wind, and the 'sheet' did the same for the other clew. The wartake seems to have helped the tack in some way.

Fig. 54. SEAL OF DANZIG, 1400

For an idea of ships of this time, 1400 or thereabouts, in the final stage of development of the one-masted rig, three illustrations, Figs. 54 and 55 and Plate IV, should be taken together. The first drawing from the seal of Danzig of the year 1400 gives a broadside view with no sail set. The plate is taken from a stained-glass window at Bourges in France. It is of rather later date, but the ship is still a one-master, and the artist was probably being old fashioned on purpose. The second drawing, the work of Mr R. Morton Nance, comes from an illustration in a French manuscript. It shows two slightly different types, which may perhaps represent a merchantman and a man-of-war, or rather a ship meant chiefly for trading and one intended mainly for fighting; the real hard and fast distinction between the man-of-war and the merchantman came at least two centuries later. The pictures

PLATE IV

SHIP ON A STAINED-GLASS WINDOW IN THE MUSEUM
AT BOURGES (1400)

explain themselves, but it may be worth noting that the merchantman in Fig. 55 has what is almost certainly a capstan in the stern.

These one-masted, clinker-built ships had been the standard type in the North for two centuries, and for

Fig. 55. SHIPS OF ABOUT 1400
From a French manuscript.   Drawn by Mr R. Morton Nance

the latter half of that time had been well known in the Mediterranean as well. In the North they had replaced the double-ended Viking type, and in the South they had to a great extent taken the place of the mediæval Mediterranean two-master, such as will be described in the next chapter. The one-master had developed as far as she could, and the clinker method of building was also very near its limits. In the fifteenth century drastic changes were introduced in both rigging and hull, and the result was in all important respects the full-rigged ship, which lasted with comparatively little change for another four hundred years or more.

CHAPTER VI

SOUTHERN SHIPS IN THE MIDDLE AGES

A.D. 400–1400

WHILE Northern ships had been progressing from the open boat of Nydam to the heavy, decked, one-masted sailing-ship of the seal of Ipswich the ships of the Mediterranean had been developing on lines of their own. In their case the improvement in the course of a thousand years or so was nothing like so great as in the North ; in fact, by the end of the period the Northern ship, although starting far behind, had outstripped her Southern rival in many respects. A proof of this is that during the fourteenth century the Northern type was taken up in the Mediterranean itself.

In the North the great event had been the introduction of the stern-rudder ; in the South it was a change of rig on a hull that remained very much the same. The Roman merchantman of A.D. 200 (Fig. 22) had a big square sail amidships and a little square sail on a mast slanting over the bows. The ordinary Mediterranean sailing-ship of 1200 had also two masts, but the foremast was the larger, and they set an entirely new kind of sail, the 'lateen.'

All sails, or at any rate all European sails, belong to one of two great classes : they are either 'square' sails or 'fore-and-aft' sails. The former hang naturally *across* the length of the ship, the latter *along* it. To make use of wind from either side of the ship the square sail has to be twisted so that sometimes one of its two ' up-and-down ' edges is nearest the wind and sometimes the other, but it always receives the wind on the same surface. Its two edges change duties, but its back is always its back and its front is always its front.

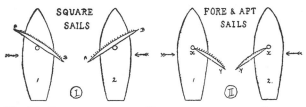

Fig. 56. DIAGRAM SHOWING DIFFERENCE BETWEEN SQUARE SAILS AND FORE-AND-AFT SAILS

The fore-and-aft sail is just the opposite in both ways. Its ' luff,' or edge nearest the wind, is always the luff, and the ' leech,' or edge away from the wind, is always the leech. On the other hand, the pressure of the wind comes sometimes on one side of its material and sometimes on the other.

This is perhaps easier to illustrate than to explain in words. In Fig. 56 I, 1 and I, 2 are bird's-eye views of a ship with a single square sail. I, 1 has the wind on the port side and I, 2 on the starboard. The two edges of the sail are marked A and B, and one side of the canvas is shown with a row of little spikes. It will be seen that this side is always away from the wind, while sometimes edge A and sometimes edge B is nearest to the point from which the wind comes. The other two drawings, II, 1 and II, 2, are similar views of a ship with one fore-and-aft sail. In this case edge X is always nearer the wind than edge Y, while the wind sometimes strikes on the spiked surface and sometimes on the other.

The next diagram (Fig. 57) shows four of the chief kinds of fore-and-aft sails : the ' lateen,' ' lug,' ' gaff-

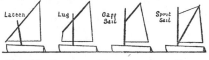

Fig. 57. TYPES OF FORE-AND-AFT SAILS

sail,' and ' spritsail.' The thick lines represent the mast and the yard, gaff, or sprit that holds up the sail. The last two types have the luff attached to the mast and have their whole area abaft the mast. The other

Fig. 58. CHINESE JUNK WITH LUG SAILS

two have a long yard, like the yard of a square sail, and have part of their surface before the mast. ' Staysails,' which form another important class of fore-and-aft sails, are shaped like lateens or like lugs and are set without yards beneath the stays leading forward and downward from the mastheads.

The lateen is the typical sail of the Mediterranean

and Red Seas. The lug is used very largely in English fishing-boats and in ships' boats, while a more complicated form with battens, or light rods, across it is the sail used in nearly all Chinese vessels (Fig. 58). The gaff-sail is the sail used in schooners and cutters, the

Fig. 59. Indian Ship of the Seventh Century

ordinary sail of most yachts. The spritsail is the sail of the Thames barge and of many Dutch small craft.

Clearly, by twisting a square sail round and lifting up one end it could be made into something not very different from a lug, but the shrouds would get in the way. This brings out another difference : the fore-and-aft sail is set inside the rigging, the square sail outside. Still, probably in a small boat with no shrouds, or perhaps even before shrouds were invented, some one may have tried doing this with a square sail when the wind was on one side and found it a success. Something of the sort is well shown in the Indian ships of the seventh century on the sculptures of Boro Budur in Java (Fig. 59), and can still be seen, or could fairly recently, in the modern Egyptian 'nugger,' with her sail very much the shape of the ancient Egyptian square sail, but set like a lug.

It is not hard to imagine how this sail might change into the real lug or the lateen, or how the gaff-sail might

be produced by cutting off the fore part of either of these, but the spritsail seems to require a separate origin. Possibly it arose from a V-shaped double mast, such as is used in many Eastern canoes. The canoes of Ceylon show this very well ; in fact it is hard to know whether they should be described as having a double mast or a mast and a sprit.

Fig. 60. LATEEN SAILS
From a Greek manuscript of about A.D. 886

Speaking roughly, the lateen is still found from Portugal to the Black Sea, in the Red Sea and Persian Gulf, on the West Coast of India, and down the East Coast of Africa as far as Zanzibar. It may be only a very strange coincidence, but it is worth noting that this is more or less the area over which the Mohammedan religion extends, or once extended. The lateen arose too, or at any rate began to spread over the Mediterranean, about the same time as Mohammedanism. The very early Middle Ages are a bad time for ship pictures, but a Greek manuscript in the Bibliothèque

Nationale in Paris (MS. *grec* 510), written about A.D. 886, shows two very obvious and well-drawn lateens. These are copied in Fig. 60. Jal's *Glossaire Nautique* has a sketch on p. 257, which is copied in Fig. 61. It is said to be from a Greek manuscript of the ninth century,

Fig. 61. LATEEN-RIGGED VESSEL OF THE NINTH CENTURY

but the reference is wrong, and this date cannot be checked. Probably the rig was invented on the Nile, like so much else in the way of shipbuilding, before the arrival of the Saracen invaders in 640, and was spread by them in the course of their more distant conquests. A sail of somewhat the same shape, but with another yard or boom along the foot, is used in the East Indies and the Pacific in craft called 'praos' (Fig. 62), and it is just a possibility that the origin of the lateen should be sought in that direction.

THE SAILING-SHIP

A Spanish manuscript of the thirteenth century shows us the two-masted lateener in her prime. The drawing (Fig. 63) is from a photograph of one of the miniatures added as a decoration to a treatise on minerals known as the *Lapidario* of King Alfonso the Wise. The picture

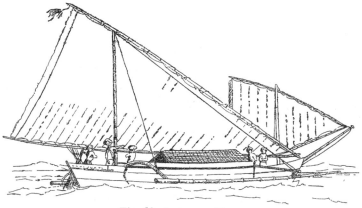

Fig. 62. JAVANESE PRAO

is small and does not show much detail, but the new type of sail is very evident, even though the artist has chosen a position in which it looks more like a square sail than usual. The lateen, by the way, is a sail that can be set in all sorts of positions. From experience with Northern sails one would think that many drawings of Southern ships show their sails set in ways that must have been invented by the artist for picturesque effect, but a visit to the Mediterranean soon does away with this idea and leaves the impression that nothing is impossible to the lateen.

The hull of this Spanish ship recalls that of the Roman merchantman. Its bow and stern are quite unlike one another—in contrast to the ships on Northern seals of about the same date, where the ship is still in most respects double-ended. The pattern on the side represents the projecting ends of two rows of deck-beams—a Southern feature found in Egyptian and in Roman vessels, but quite unknown in the North. The large square between the two decks is a port for loading cargo ; this we shall see again in much later Southern ships.

The deck-beams and the great side-rudders are shown far better in the photograph (Plate I) from a copy at South Kensington of the shrine of St Peter the Martyr, in Milan. This is work of 1340, when Northern designs had begun to influence Medi-terranean shipbuilding, but, even so, it is one of the most

Fig. 63. TWO-MASTED LATEENER FROM THE *LAPIDARIO* OF ALFONSO THE WISE

valuable records of Southern ships of the Middle Ages. Some of the peculiarities of Southern rigging will be mentioned later on in this chapter. At the moment it will be enough to call attention to the way in which the mast slopes, or rakes, forward. This was nearly always the case in lateen-rigged ships. Probably the sail is not strictly a lateen, but a ' settee,' which was a sail between the true lateen and the lug. Drawings of this period show all three types shading into one another, and it is hard to know how to classify some specimens. One thing is certain, this is a fore-and-aft sail and not a square sail.

The two-masted lateen rig has lasted up to the pre-sent day, though not in ships of very great size. A ' tartane ' from a French book of 1710 (Fig. 64) shows a kind of vessel that was then common in the Mediterranean. Nowadays the 'tartana' is a one-master with a lateen mainsail and a 'jib,' or triangular stay-sail, instead of the lateen foresail. Most Mediterranean lateeners now carry a jib, even if they are still two-masters, and to find the home of the old-fashioned rig of two lateens only it is necessary to go to the Red Sea

Fig. 64. TARTANE OF 1710

or the Persian Gulf among the many kinds of craft that Europeans lump together as 'dhows.' The 'garukha' from the Persian Gulf shown in Fig. 65 was taken from a sketch made as long ago as 1838, but almost exactly similar vessels are still common, and some of them still have the peculiar steering-gear shown in the sketch, a pair of more or less complicated tackles leading from a spar on each quarter to the back of the rudder.

Besides the two-masted lateener there seems to have been in the Mediterranean in the twelfth and thirteenth centuries a two-masted square-sailed type, differing from the other in rig only, and probably a direct descendant of the late Roman ship shown in Fig. 23. One-masted lateeners were no doubt common, and we know that such things as three-masters did exist.

106

Such a ship was the great Saracen ' dromon ' with which Richard I fought in 1191 on his way to the Third Crusade. We know very little about her except that she was a sailing-ship with three masts and was much bigger than the ordinary ships of her time. We

Fig. 65. GARUKHA OF 1838

do not know definitely whether she carried square sails or lateens, though the latter is much the more likely. Still, the action is interesting because it is one of the comparatively few occasions when a king of England has commanded in a naval battle. For a long time little could be done against her ; the English did manage to board her after they had disabled her steering-gear, but they were driven back with heavy loss. In the end she was sunk by being rammed again and again by the galleys.

Strictly speaking, the name ' dromon ' belonged to the oared fighting-ships of the Eastern Roman Empire.

These big galleys had two rows of twenty-five oars each on either side. A ship of this kind is shown, not very clearly, in another Spanish thirteenth-century manuscript (Fig. 66). Names of ships have a way of meaning one thing at one date and something quite different at

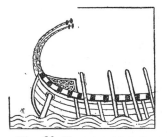

Fig. 66. DROMON OF THE THIRTEENTH CENTURY

another. The 'frigate' of Nelson's time had no possible resemblance to the mediæval Mediterranean 'fregata,' except perhaps in the purpose for which she was used. The present-day 'galeass' of the Baltic, a ship very like an English coasting-ketch, has even less connexion with the 'galeazza' of the battle of Lepanto or the Spanish Armada, while the name 'mahon,' which is what the Turks called the galeass, is now used by them for a sort of harbour barge.

At the time of the Crusades the Mediterranean was no longer under single control, as it had been in Roman times. The Western Empire had fallen, and on its ruins had arisen a number of independent states of varying size and importance. Some of the smallest on land were the most important at sea. Three of them, the Italian republics of Genoa, Pisa, and Venice, with Marseilles in France, and Barcelona in Spain, accounted for by far the greater part of the Christian shipping in the Mediterranean. Accordingly, when Louis IX of France undertook the Ninth Crusade he turned to Venice and Genoa for ships. Fortunately, some of the agreements made in 1268 for the hire of these ships have been preserved. They give many details of the measurements of a number of Venetian ships, and tell us something of the masts, sails, and rigging of some of the Genoese.

In both cases some ships were to be built specially for the expedition. The Venetians were to be 58 feet long on the keel, or 86 feet from stem to sternpost, including the rake at each end. They were to be 21½ feet wide, 22 feet deep from the keel to the bulwarks amidships, and to have their stem and sternpost rising 29 feet above the keel. They were to have two complete decks, with a half-deck above them from the middle of the ship to the bows, and

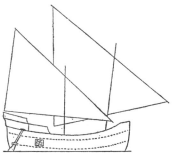

Fig. 67. Sail-plan of Venetian Ship of 1268

with two or three extra decks forming cabins in the stern.

The new Genoese ships were to be rather smaller: 75 feet long over all, as against 86. The chief interest about them is that we know the lengths of their masts and yards. The foremast was 76½ feet long—just more than the total length of the ship; the 'middle-mast' was 60½ feet. Their yards, allowing for the overlap of the two parts of which they were made, were 96 feet and 84 feet long. Both were therefore longer than the ship, and must have stuck out over the bow and stern when lowered.

If the Venetians were rigged on about the same proportions, as no doubt they were, they must have been something like the diagram given in Fig. 67. Such ships were still to be seen in the Mediterranean nearly two hundred years later. The Western states had taken to the square rig long before, but the Turks continued to use big lateeners like the ship in Fig. 68, which is taken from a German account of a voyage to Jerusalem about the middle of the fifteenth century.

While the Crusades were actually going on the

Fig. 68. TURKISH SHIP OF THE FIFTEENTH CENTURY

Northern type of ship seems to have been only a visitor in the Mediterranean. With the fourteenth century it came in to stay. A Florentine writer puts its arrival in the year 1304, when people from Bayonne, in the southwest corner of France, near the Pyrenees, came into the Mediterranean as pirates in ships called 'cogs.' The merchants of Genoa, Venice, and Barcelona took up the new type at once, and it soon began to displace the two-masted lateener.

This great change, from two masts to one, from the lateen to the square sail, and from the two side-rudders to the stern-rudder, is shown by a comparison of the ship in Fig. 63 with one of those from another Spanish manuscript, which was finished in 1388. The subject is the Trojan War; but the artist, as always happened in those days, drew the ships and the costumes of his own time. As far as one can judge from a picture which shows little detail (Fig. 69), the ship looks very much the same as a Northerner of the same date.

In spite of the change in shape and in rig, there were some Southern features which survived. Roman ships and early Southern mediæval ships were carvel-built, with their planks fitted edge to edge instead of overlapping like those of the clinker-built ships of the North. Southern rigging

Fig. 69. MEDITERRANEAN SHIP TOWARD THE END OF THE FOURTEENTH CENTURY

had also its peculiarities. In the North the shrouds were attached to the mast in or above the topcastle, while the holes, or ' hounds,' for the ' ties ' which hoisted the yard were well below it. In the South the opposite was the case : the shrouds started from below the top, if there was one, and the ties went through what was called a ' calcet,' a square block of wood at the extreme head of the mast. Fig. 70 shows these differences. There was also another difference about the shrouds. In the North they were single ropes down to about the line of the ship's side and were set up, or tightened, by means of thin ' laniards ' which passed through holes in ' deadeyes ' at the ends of the shrouds and in a platform, called the ' chainwale,' secured to the side of the ship. In the South they acted only as ' pendants,' or short fixed ropes carrying blocks for tackles of various kinds. Thus it was possible in Northern ships to stretch 'ratlines' across from shroud to shroud to form a rope ladder for going aloft, but in Southern ships a separate rope ladder with wooden rungs had to be fitted close up to the mast. Later on, about the end of the fifteenth century, the Southern

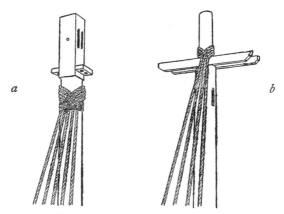

Fig. 70. DIAGRAM SHOWING DIFFERENCES BETWEEN (*a*) SOUTHERN AND (*b*) NORTHERN MASTHEADS

method of building and the Northern fashion in rigging became the rule all over Europe, but in the fourteenth, in spite of a general resemblance in appearance, these differences were always found.

About the same time as the arrival of the Northern type of sailing-ship in the Mediterranean there came also a change in the galley. Instead of the dromon, with her two rows of oars one above the other, there arose another type of bireme, in which the pairs of oars were no longer at two different levels, but were rowed by two men sitting side by side on the same thwart, or 'bank,' and acted against two thole pins close together at the same level. It was, in fact, a return to the system of the Greek vessels shown in Figs. 17 and 18. Soon there were triremes on the same system, with three men on a bank rowing separate oars in groups of three. Such a trireme was called in Italy a *galia sottil*, while the bireme took the name of *fusta*.

The arrangement of the oars and rowers in these galleys can be seen in Fig. 71, which is based on drawings of a model in Venice made in 1881 by Admiral Fincati, and is probably very close to the truth. The rowers sat on either side of a narrow raised gangway called the 'corsia,' while the thole pins against which the oars worked were set along the outer edge of the straight overhanging structure called the

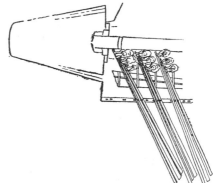

Fig. 71. Diagram showing Rowers and Oars of a Mediæval Trireme

'apostis.' If planks were laid all along the outriggers of a modern eight-oared racing-boat the result would be much the same on a small scale. At each end of these long outriggers there was a heavy cross-beam, or 'yoke.' The space before the fore-yoke was the fighting-platform, that abaft the after-yoke was the poop for the officers.

The groups of oars appear very clearly in a drawing in an early fifteenth-century Italian manuscript in the British Museum (Fig. 72). This is probably a long-voyage merchant galley, such as used to come every year to England. The hull is not straight enough for a fighting galley, and the three masts would be very unusual in that kind of vessel. Her usual rig was one very big mast and a little one. The smaller mast was at first somewhere between the mainmast and the stern, but later on was shifted to the forecastle. In either case the mainmast was so very much the more important

Fig. 72. MERCHANT GALLEY OF THE FIFTEENTH CENTURY

that usually it is the only mast shown. This is the case in the fine galley (Fig. 73) in one of Carpaccio's paintings in Venice; the mainmast and mainsail are shown in great detail, while the other mast, if there was one, is left out altogether.

Strictly speaking, this galley, having been painted about 1485, does not belong to the period of this chapter. However, galleys were changing very little, and the use of this picture to illustrate the description of a galley of the previous century is not the serious matter that such a thing would be in the case of a sailing-ship. If a seaman of the end of the fourteenth century could have returned to life after a hundred years he would have found little that was new about

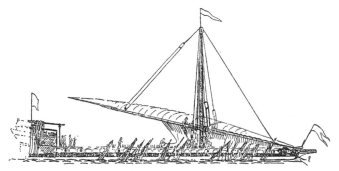

Fig. 73. Venetian Galley of the Fifteenth Century

galleys, but he would have been utterly bewildered by the changes in sailing-ships; for the fifteenth century, and more particularly its first half, was the time when the development of the sailing-ship went on at a faster pace than at any other period in history.

CHAPTER VII

THE RISE OF THE FULL-RIGGED SHIP
A.D. 1400–1600

AT the beginning of the fifteenth century the big seagoing sailing-ship had one mast and one sail. Fifty years later she had three masts and five or six sails. Unfortunately this great change comes just at a time when we are very badly off for pictures or descriptions of ships. English inventories of 1410–12 have been published, and these give a little light on the first stage of the change, but after that comes darkness. Other inventories of about 1425 are known to exist, but they have not yet been copied and printed.

The documents of 1410–12 show that one ship in the English Royal Navy—and only one—had more than one mast; she had " 1 mast magn." and " 1 mast parv."—in other words, one big mast and one small mast. The latter may have been on the forecastle as a foremast, on the aftercastle as a ' mizzen,' or even in the top as a topmast. We are not told which, but the reference is very important as being the first evidence of a second mast in Northern waters.

It must be noted that this small mast was found in a ship called the ' carake,' and a carrack was by origin a Mediterranean type. Probably she had been bought from Southern owners, and if so there can be little doubt that the small mast was what we should call

116

nowadays a mizzen, carried between the mainmast and the stern, for Southern ships at the end of the fourteenth century were certainly more likely to have their smaller mast aft than the other way about.

Plate V, from a miniature in a manuscript written for King Henry VI about 1430, gives a picture of a ship very like what the carake must have been. The hull is clearly Southern in origin, and the two masts, big and small, are well shown. There is no need to suppose that this is an actual portrait of the original carake of the 1410–12 lists, for several Genoese carracks had been captured in 1416 and 1417, and the type must have been becoming quite well known in the North by the ordinary process of trade.

Another interesting point about these lists is that some ships carried guns, though never more than three. This is, however, not quite the first evidence of the use of guns afloat. A French fleet in 1356 had a few guns, a big gun was used in action on board a Spanish ship in 1359, and both Genoese and Venetians seem to have used guns in the course of their war of 1379–80.

The name ' carrack ' was not new. It occurs in Spanish documents before the end of the thirteenth century, and there is an account of the capture by Spanish galleys in 1359 of a large Venetian carrack; but it is in the fifteenth century that the carrack was in her prime, and we see her then as a three-masted ship developed by the Southern nations from the Northern one-master and then taken up all over Europe. Genoa was the chief port from which carracks came to England, and Southampton was their harbour at this end. Every year " carrakes of Janne," or Genoa, came to Southampton laden with Mediterranean produce—

wine, oil, fruit, spices, and the like—and went home with English wool. There were Venetian carracks as well, but usually the vessels from Venice were galleys of a special type such as that shown in Fig. 71, designed and equipped for long voyages and cargo-carrying.

It was the people of Bayonne who are said to have introduced the Northern type of ship to the Mediterranean, and they seem to have had a share in the opposite process in the case of the carrack. Henry V ordered a big ship there for his Navy, and she was probably a specimen of the new carrack type. This ship was never added to the Royal Navy, for the King's ships were all sold on his death in 1422, and this ship was no doubt sold as well, if she was ever finished. Very likely she never was finished, for a report of 1419 describes her keel as being rotten when she was only about half built. This report gives her dimensions as 112 feet on the keel, 186 feet over all, and 46 feet wide. She was thus nothing like as long as Canute's great ship, though she was probably very much wider and deeper, but she was as big as anything that was built in England after her time until the end of the seventeenth century.

We know nothing of her rig. The letter speaks of "the mast beam," but that proves nothing. Neither a foremast nor a mizzen would have been more than a very small spar stepped in one of the castles at the ends. The mainmast was *the* mast, and indeed we still say 'before the mast,' as if there were only one. This helps to explain why two-masters never became common in the North. The position of the mainmast was fixed by centuries of experience, and a small mast either forward or aft would upset the balance of the sail-plan and

PLATE V

PLATE VI

Two-masted Ship from King Henry VI's
Psalter (1425)

Mediterranean Carrack, from a
German Drawing (1460)

PLATE VII

NORTHERN THREE-MASTED SHIPS (1450)
From a manuscript belonging to Lord Hastings

would at once demand a third mast to put things right. English seals of the beginning of the fifteenth century, such as that of 1417 shown in Fig. 74, show three flagstaffs, in the bow, in the stern, and in the top. Nothing could be more natural than to try setting sails on them, and thus turn them into foremast, mizzen, and top-

Fig. 74. ENGLISH SEAL OF 1417   Fig. 75. SEAL OF LOUIS DE
BOURBON, 1466

mast. That probably is how every mast except the mainmast originated.

The first actual dated three-masted ship known at present is on a seal of Louis de Bourbon, belonging to 1466 (Fig. 75). It is certain, though, that there were such ships a good deal earlier, and there are good examples of them in a manuscript which belongs to Lord Hastings and is believed to be not later than 1450. These ships, as can be seen in Plate VII, have a spritsail for setting under the bowsprit (quite a distinct sail from the fore-and-aft spritsail), a square foresail and mainsail, and a lateen mizzen ; most of them show or suggest a main topsail, and one—the ship in the top left hand corner   has a fore topsail as well. The hulls show long overhanging forecastles, with aftercastles reduced in height but lengthened as far as the mainmast. The great interest of these ships is the wonderful development they show. It is not exaggeration to say that a man who could handle them would not have had much to learn before being able to take charge of a ship of Nelson's day, or even of a little later.

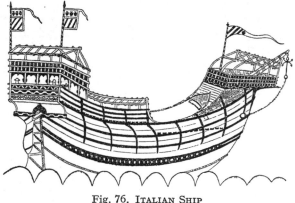

Fig. 76. ITALIAN SHIP
About 1450

In other words, the full-rigged ship had arrived, and was to remain the same in essentials for about four hundred years.

The hulls of two Italian carracks of about the same date as these English ships are drawn in the same manuscript as the galley in Fig. 72. The ship of 1000 ' botte ' (about five hundred tons) is shown in Fig. 76. She was 85 feet long on the keel, or about 125 feet from stem to sternpost, and 34 feet wide. The ends of the deck-beams are shown in Southern style, and we can see that the upper deck dropped suddenly amidships. The awning across instead of along the poop is a typical carrack touch, and so is the sloping bulkhead with an arched opening in it beneath the forecastle.

THE FULL-RIGGED SHIP

One of the finest ship-drawings of this or of any previous century is the 'kraeck,' or carrack, drawn about 1470 by the artist who signed his pictures "W.A." It has been shown by Mr Morton Nance in his book on *Sailing-ship Models* that some points about this drawing suggest that it was made from a model. If so the model-maker deserves our gratitude as much as the artist, for the result of their joint efforts is splendid. The print, copied in Fig. 77, shows a ship of distinctly Southern origin; the rope ladder up the mast proves that, but the shrouds, although they have no ratlines across them, are set up in Northern fashion, with deadeyes, or 'deadmen's eyes,' as they were called in those days. The gallery in the stern is a new feature, and so are the guns which can be seen peeping out under the half-deck just at the foot of the mizzen, while a 'hand-gun' in the mizzentop is very conspicuous. Other points of interest are the grapnel under the bowsprit, the ammunition-hoists from the deck to the foretop and maintop, and the 'parrels,' or gigantic bead necklaces, by which the yards were held close to the masts and at the same time allowed to run up and down easily. Plate VI shows a bow view of a similar ship from a German manuscript of about the same date. This ship is more Southern still; she has all her yards made of two pieces lashed together in true lateen-yard fashion. This is not surprising, because she appears to be a Turk.

There are other good pictures of ships of the latter half of the fifteenth century in the well-known life of the Earl of Warwick. This is not Richard Neville, "the King-maker," but his father-in-law, Richard Beauchamp, who died in 1439. However, the life does not seem to have been written till about 1490, so the ships are probably not of much earlier date than that.

Fig. 77. CARRACK OF ABOUT 1470

Some of them show four masts, the fourth being an after-mizzen. Heavy guns appear amidships, firing over the bulwarks.

To confirm these pictures we can turn to actual inventories of the reign of Henry VII. The *Grâce Dieu* in 1485, then an old ship, had four masts. She had a mainsail with three bonnets and a main topsail, a foresail with two bonnets, two mizzen-sails (main mizzen and after-mizzen), and a spritsail with a bonnet. Three of her masts had tops, she carried twenty-one guns, a great boat, and a bell, and her shrouds were set up with deadeyes. This ship was broken up in 1486 and her materials used for the *Sovereign*, which in 1495 had a mainmast with top and topmast, a foremast with top and topmast, a mizzenmast with a top, and a 'bonaventure-mast,' or after-mizzen. She had 31 guns and 110 'serpentines,' these being very light guns mounted in the castles. The *Regent* at the same date was even more elaborately rigged. She had a top to her main topmast, with a mast and sail above that—what was called a 'topgallant sail' later on. She had also a fore topmast and tops to both her mizzenmasts. The *Santa Maria*, in which Columbus discovered America in 1492, was an ordinary three-masted ship with spritsail, foresail, mainsail, main topsail, and mizzen.

The *Santa Maria* is often called a 'caravel.' She was nothing of the sort; she was a perfectly normal square-rigged ship. Of Columbus' other two vessels the *Pinta* seems to have been built as a caravel, but to have been re-rigged as a ship before he had anything to do with her, while the *Niña* started as a caravel and was altered on the way. The origin of the word 'caravel' is very uncertain, but the type of vessel seems to have been a Portuguese form of the lateener. It was a fairly small vessel with three lateen sails, the biggest forward and the smallest aft. Apparently its stern above the waterline was finished off square, instead of having the side-planking brought round in the ordinary way. A ship of this sort appears on a Spanish map of 1500 (Fig. 78) which is said to be the work of one of the companions of Columbus.

In the second half of the fifteenth century we meet 'carvels' in the North. Sometimes, particularly at

first, this may have meant a Southern caravel, or a ship of similar rig, but more usually it indicated a ship with flush planking, or carvel-built. Up to then Northern ships had been almost always clinker-built, with overlapping planks. The new fashion started in Brittany, and it is quite possible that it may have survived there since the days of the Veneti, at any rate in

Fig. 78. CARAVEL FROM A SPANISH MAP OF 1500

small craft. It was introduced to Holland in 1459, and it soon became general. It is said that 'carvel' and 'caravel' are really quite distinct words, but the confusion between them goes back almost as far as the words themselves, and it seems that the square stern of the caravel appeared as another new feature of the carvel build. Certainly square sterns did become general just about this date.

Two famous ships that were definitely called carvels were the *Peter* of La Rochelle, which came to Danzig in 1462, and the Swedish man-of-war *Elefant*, built in 1532. Each of these was known in her day as "the great carvel." The first was 150 feet long from stem to sternpost and 42 feet wide, the second was 174 feet long and 40 feet wide.

The early part of the sixteenth century was a time when it was thought necessary in every country to have one enormous ship. The Scottish *Great Michael* of 1511 was followed by the English *Henry Grâce à Dieu* in 1514. The French, after buying the *Great Michael*, tried to go one better and produced the *Grand François* in 1527, while the Swedes built the *Elefant* in 1532, as has been mentioned already. In the South the two outstanding ships were the great carrack *Santa Anna*, built for the Knights of Malta in 1523, and the Portuguese *São João* of 1534. The *Great Michael* is said to have been 240 feet long over all, the *Elefant* was 239 feet. For the others we have no precise dimensions— only such information as that a man in the uppermost of the four tops on the mainmast of the *Grand François* looked no bigger than a chicken. This particular ship had a thoroughly exaggerated rig with five masts. She never got to sea, but was wrecked in harbour before she was finished ; the others all took part in actual warlike operations.

The *Henry Grâce à Dieu* had topsails and topgallant sails on her first three masts and a topsail to the bonaventure mizzen. The mizzen topsails were lateens like the sails below them. She was built up to a great height at each end, having eight decks one above the other in her stern, and she carried 184 guns, mostly small. There is no good picture of this ship, though there are two which show her as she looked after a complete ' rebuild ' in 1536–39.

The big Portuguese ship was called a ' galleon.' It is not easy to define this new type, and it is made harder by the fact that the same ship might be called a galley, a galleon, a galeass, and a bark. The usual idea is that a galleon must be Spanish and very high out of the water. This is certainly wrong, for even if

Spain or Portugal was its home it was very soon found
in Northern waters as well. The word ought to mean
a large galley, but this it never did. The galley was
meant purely and simply for fighting under oars, while
the galleon probably never carried oars at all. As far as
one can judge, the galleon was a sailing-ship—usually
four-masted—with the ordinary ship-rig of the time,
but with a hull built to some extent on galley lines,

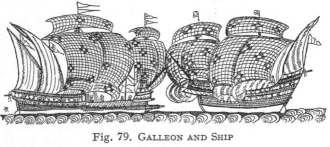

Fig. 79. GALLEON AND SHIP
About 1550

long for its beam, rather straight and flat, and with
a beak-head low down like a galley's, instead of the
overhanging forecastle of the ship. This difference is
shown very well in the drawing in Fig. 79 from the lid
of a chest belonging to Lord Berkeley. The older ship
type may also be seen in Fig. 80, which is taken from
a Spanish map of 1529.

There are several pictures of the *São João,* all showing
her at the attack on Tunis in 1535. Of those copied here
the first (Fig. 81) is from one of the tapestries woven
to celebrate the expedition, the other from a set of
paintings on the walls of a small room in the Alhambra
in Spain (Fig. 82). Another drawing from this last
source (Fig. 83) gives two caravels and shows how this
type had developed into a four-master, square-rigged

on the foremast only. Unfortunately these paintings have suffered so much from neglect and misuse that they show hardly any detail.

The *São João* is said to have carried no fewer than 366 guns. This is not impossible if the hand-guns are included, for the actual inventory of the *Henry Grâce à*

Fig. 80. SHIP FROM A SPANISH MAP OF 1529

Dieu shows that she had 384 guns on the same method of counting.

Somewhere about the end of the fifteenth century there had come an important change in the arrangement of ships' guns. Up to now they had been carried on the upper deck, firing over or through the bulwarks, while the lighter pieces had been carried in the castles at each end. The change was that the heavier guns were now put between decks and that ports were cut for them in the actual side of the ship. This invention is usually ascribed to the year 1501 and to a Frenchman.

127

THE SAILING-SHIP

Certainly one of the first drawings showing guns between decks is French and belongs to the first ten years of the sixteenth century. It is a drawing of the *Louise*, which was flagship of the French Mediterranean

Fig. 81. PORTUGUESE GALLEON, 1535
From the Madrid Tapestries

fleet. As a drawing, it has been shown to be mainly a copy from an earlier design, but the most definite original touch about it is the presence of two guns pointing through holes in the side amidships. After this guns between decks become common; they are found in the well-known picture of the embarkation of Henry VIII at Dover in 1520, and the *São João* in 1535 shows them very clearly (Fig. 81).

THE FULL-RIGGED SHIP

Up to now a sea-fight had been really a matter of land-fighting at sea. One ship could damage another only by ramming, and the best way of settling things was to get alongside, lash the ships together, and fight it out hand to hand with the aid of lime-pots, stones,

Fig. 82. PORTUGUESE GALLEON, 1535
From the Alhambra paintings

and spears from the tops, and of the small guns in the castles. With the arrival of heavy guns it became possible to disable an enemy from a distance. A ship was actually sunk by gun-fire in 1513, but heavy guns were slow and uncertain, and right up to the end of the century we still find the old-fashioned weapons in the lists. After all, hand-to-hand fighting was always a possibility that had to be allowed for. Even in the late War, when gun ranges could be reckoned in miles, there was a case of boarding in the old style.

Very soon after the carrying of guns between decks became general the guns themselves began to change. The slow, clumsy breech-loader that had to be taken to pieces each time for reloading was replaced by a far simpler and more convenient muzzle-loader of a type that altered very little for another three hundred years.

Plate VIII shows the *Henry Grâce à Dieu* in her rebuilt form, in which she was really a new ship carrying 21 heavy brass guns, 130 iron guns, and 100 hand-guns. In her case it will be seen that there

Fig. 83. PORTUGUᴇSE CARAVELS, 1535

was already a second row of ports in the hull proper. This drawing is one of the series in *A Declaration of the Royal Navy* presented to the King in 1546 by Anthony Anthony, an officer of the Ordnance. He was not a great draughtsman, but his duties would have given him a chance to know how ships carried their guns, and his pictures differ enough for us to believe that they were meant for real portraits.

A much better drawn picture of a smaller ship is given in Fig. 84 from a plan of Calais drawn in 1541. Both this and the *Henry Grâce à Dieu* show vessels of the ship type, with the projecting forecastle rather than the low-lying beak of the galleon. Such a beak is shown as a contrast in another drawing from Anthony Anthony, the 'galeass' *Hart* (Fig. 85).

This introduces another new type, an attempt to

130

PLATE VIII

THE *HENRY GRÁCE À DIEU* (1545)

combine the good points of the sailing-ship and the galley. In the South it was more galley than ship, lateen-rigged, except for a small square sail on the fore-mast and carrying its big guns forward like a galley. In

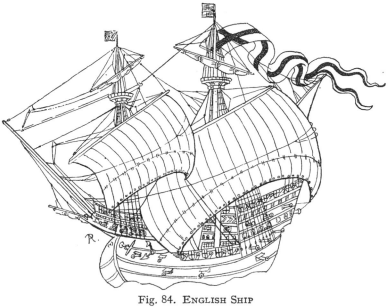

Fig. 84. ENGLISH SHIP
About 1540

the North it carried its guns along the broadside, with small ports for oars below them, and had the ordinary square rig. A Scottish description of 1549 speaks of a galeass as setting the usual sails of a ship together with 'studding-sails,' which were extras stuck out at the sides of the other sails. She had also "a hundred oars on every side"—plainly meaning only a very large number. Two Scottish galeasses were captured by the English in 1544, and one of them had been given to James V by the King of France in 1537, so it may be that it was the French, with their two coasts, who first introduced this type to the North.

Henry VIII took it up keenly. He had already made one striking attempt to combine the sailing-ship and the galley in a big vessel launched in 1515 and called the

Fig. 85. ENGLISH GALEASS
About 1545

Great Galley. This galeass, as the Venetian ambassadors called her, was a four-master with a foresail and fore topsail, a mainsail, topsail, and topgallant sail, and two mizzens, one with a topsail. She rowed sixty oars on each side and had 70 brass and 147 iron guns. Probably she was about 180 feet long without her beak-head. One remarkable feature about her is that she was clinker-built; at least we are told that in 1523 they had " to break her up and make her carvel . . . for she was the dangeroust ship under water that ever man sailed in." In the end she was rebuilt as an ordinary sailing-ship and usually called the *Great Barke.*

THE FULL-RIGGED SHIP

In the war of 1545 the French galleys from the Mediterranean were opposed by the new English galeasses and by ' rowbarges '—small, square-rigged vessels pulling sixteen oars a side. None of these craft, galeasses, galleys, or rowbarges, lasted long in the North ; by the

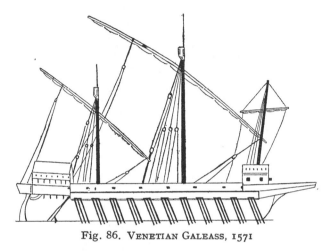

Fig. 86. VENETIAN GALEASS, 1571

end of the century they had vanished, and the sailing-ship was left supreme.

Conditions were different in the Mediterranean. There the galley remained the standard fighting vessel. Sailing-ships were looked on more as transports than as men-of-war, and it was the galeass that supported the galleys if required. This was the case at the great battle of Lepanto in 1571, where the Turks, for the first time in history, were thoroughly beaten by the combined fleets of Spain, Venice, and the Pope. In this battle there were more than two hundred galleys engaged on either side. Fig. 86 is an attempt to combine in a diagram several rather unsatisfactory portraits of the Venetian galeasses which were one of the strong points of the Christian fleet.

133

THE SAILING-SHIP

Soon after this there came a change in the method of rowing. Attempts to improve the trireme by adding a

Fig. 87. FLEMISH MAN-OF-WAR
About 1565

fourth, and even a fifth, oar to each bank had proved a failure, and in the end every country adopted the simpler method of having longer, heavier oars and putting several men, usually five, to each oar. With this change, and with the shifting of the mainmast far enough aft to allow of a foremast nearly as big, the Mediterranean galley reached her final form.

As a result of all this experimenting in the early part of the sixteenth century ships began to be really seaworthy. They could go to sea and stay there for either peaceful or warlike purposes. Naval warfare in the past had been little more than the transport of soldiers across the sea ; now it began to be a business in itself. Trade and discovery gained by the improvement in ships, and at the same time provided a reason

Fig. 88. FLEMISH MERCHANTMAN
About 1565

for the improvement to be maintained. Twenty years of English trading and fighting in the Indies in spite of the claims of Spain and Portugal had their climax, in 1577–80, in Drake's famous voyage round the world. During this voyage he went from Java to Sierra Leone, at least 8500 miles, without touching at any port on the way. Seaworthiness and seamanship had indeed been attained.

For an idea of ships such as Drake and his contemporaries used we can turn to the work of Brueghel, a Flemish artist who drew a series of ships about 1565. Fig. 87 shows a man-of-war, and Fig. 88 a round-

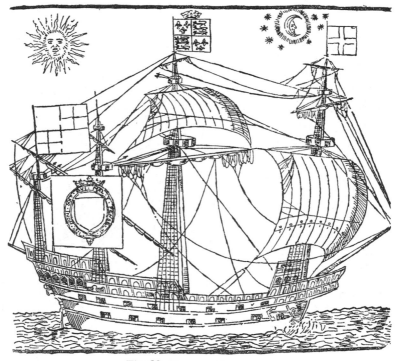

Fig. 89. ENGLISH SHIP, 1574

sterned merchantman of a type that became famous in the next century, the 'fluyt,' in which the Dutch carried on half the trade of Europe.

The next drawing (Fig. 89), from the title-page of a book printed in 1574, shows one of the larger ships with which the English defeated the Spanish Armada, while another title-page (Fig. 90), from a book printed at Barcelona in 1592, shows a big Spanish ship. This is interesting for the way in which the main-yard is shown lowered on to the bulwarks. Finally, a Dutch print of 1594 by Barentsoen, copied in Fig. 91, gives

Fig. 90. SPANISH SHIP, 1592

us a really large Northern man-of-war of the end of the century. In this and the English ship we see balconies built across the stern and on the ship's side near the stern. These are the stern and 'quarter' galleries, which started as mere conveniences, but developed during the seventeenth century into one of the chief beauties of a ship.

137

Turn back to the seal of Danzig (Fig. 54), and the change is enormous, but turn to the ships of Lord Hastings' manuscript (Plate VII) and there are more resemblances than differences. The hull is longer and

Fig. 91. DUTCH SHIP, 1594

more built up at the ends, though the forecastle has already begun to drop again ; its greatest height came early in the sixteenth century. The beak-head, one of the marks of a galleon, is a new feature, and so are the gun-ports, now shown in two complete rows.

Rigging has not changed at all in essentials. There is sometimes a fourth mast, and there are extra top-sails and topgallant sails, but the principle of two square-rigged masts forward and of lateens aft is still untouched.

Decoration had perhaps increased, for ships of Elizabeth's reign had all their upper works painted in bright colours and striking patterns, but it had by no means reached its height. That came in the next century, when the art of the woodcarver was employed to such an extent that ships became more beautiful than at any time before or since.

CHAPTER VIII

THE SEVENTEENTH CENTURY

THE two centuries covered in the last chapter included a short period of very rapid change, and after that a long spell of slow development. This chapter will see the development continued without any great change at all. There are three excuses for devoting a whole chapter to one comparatively uneventful century: it was a time when ships reached their greatest beauty, when the characteristics of the ships of different countries were specially noticeable, and when, for the first time, we get reliable portraits of particular ships.

The first illustration (Plate IX) is not one of these portraits, but a fancy picture of a large man-of-war ' invented and drawn ' early in the century by a Danish artist who evidently tried to give his ship everything possible in the way of splendid decoration and elaborate rigging. In many ways this ship is well in advance of the Dutch ship in Fig. 91. The hull shows a much straighter line, the piled-up forecastle has gone, and the beak-head has dropped till it lies nearly horizontal. In the rigging the most conspicuous change is that the bowsprit has a top at its end with a topmast and a furled sail. This sail, the ' spritsail topsail,' is one of the chief marks of a seventeenth-century ship. Its origin is plain enough—it grew from a flagstaff, like other masts. What is not plain is why such an awkward and

PLATE IX

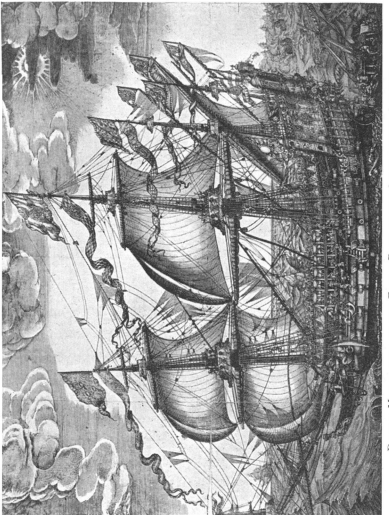

DANISH MAN-OF-WAR OF THE EARLY PART OF THE SEVENTEENTH CENTURY
Probably an imaginary vessel

PLATE X

THE *PRINCE ROYAL* (1620)

inefficient little sail should have been taken up every-where and should have lasted as it did for more than a century. The answer must be that some extra sail right forward was wanted to make up for the effect of the wind on the high poop now that there was no high forecastle to act as a balance. The spritsail is furled in position and no longer brought into the head. There are still lateen mizzen topsails, and there may have been a main mizzen topgallant sail. The most surprising thing is the hint of a sail above the main topgallant sail. It is only a hint, for there is neither sail nor yard, but the slack ropes beneath the flagstaff-stay can only be bowlines ready for a sail that might be sent up if required.

Leaving this question for the moment, we come to a famous English ship, the *Prince Royal*, launched in 1610. She was designed by one of the first shipbuilders of whom we know much apart from his work, Phineas Pett, descendant of a family of shipbuilders and an educated man as well, able to combine mathematical calculation with the rules of practical experience.

Every book on the history of ships gives a picture of the *Prince Royal*, and never by any chance is it a true one. They are all copied from one of two sources: a plate in Charnock's *History of Naval Architecture* of 1801 or a painting at Trinity House, and both of these are ships of a much later date. The best genuine portrait of this ship is reproduced in Plate X from a painting by Vroom, at Haarlem in Holland. Another by the same artist at Hampton Court has unfortunately lost a good deal of its value by being restored.

There are two important points about the Haarlem picture. It shows three complete rows of gun-ports;

the lower-deck ports are shut, those on the middle deck are open, and the upper-deck guns point through round decorated holes. Another change has come to the rigging : the lateen topsails to the mizzens have

Fig. 92. ENGLISH MERCHANTMAN
About 1620.   From a model

been replaced by square topsails like those on the other masts. The square mizzen topsail had to have a second yard to spread its foot, and in this particular picture there are furled sails beneath those yards as well. It is doubtful if this is correct ; it may have been tried when the yard was first introduced, but it never became the fashion, and, in fact, this yard, which we called the ' cross-jack ' or ' crojack ' yard, was known by the

French as the *vergue sèche,* or barren yard, because it set no sail of its own.

Merchantmen, which were usually quite small and had few men to spare, could not go in for so much complication of rigging and were slower in taking up the new mizzen topsail and the spritsail topsail. Their usual rig would still be that of a hundred and fifty years earlier : spritsail, foresail, fore topsail, mainsail, main topsail, and lateen mizzen. Some idea of a small merchantman of the beginning of the seventeenth century is given by the sketch (Fig. 92) from a model designed by one of the writers of this book to show, as nearly as possible, the appearance of the *Mayflower,* in which the Pilgrim Fathers crossed to America in 1620.

Fig. 93. STERN OF DUTCH FLUYT, 1640

Side by side with this type of merchantman there was the Dutch fluyt, with her remarkable stern of the shape shown in Fig. 93, fat and round near the water and thin and flat higher up. This was the time when the Dutch, while still fighting against Spanish rule, were rapidly getting the sea-borne trade of Europe into their hands, and it was largely in these fluyts that this trade was carried on.

It is a curious thing that England, where the round-sterned fluyt type was never really common, was the first country to break away from the flat, square stern which had been universal in big ships since about 1500. Right through the second half of the seventeenth century the great feature that more than any other marked off English ships from foreigners was the shape of the stern. All other nations stuck to the flat transom stern, the *spiegel*, or looking-glass, as the Dutch called it, while in England there came in a new design in which the planking of the bottom was brought up and round, and the stern did not become square till about ten feet or so above the waterline. It was a good deal squarer than the old stern of the fourteenth and fifteenth centuries, but it was round in comparison with the foreign stern of its own time.

This 'round-tuck' stern was well established for big ships by the middle of the seventeenth century. Apparently the famous *Sovereign of the Seas* was built with it in 1637. This ship, Phineas Pett's second great design, was a big advance in shipbuilding. She was equally remarkable for her great size, her heavy armament, and her elaborate decoration. She was not as big as Henry V's unfinished ship of 1419, but she was much bigger than anything that had been built for some years. Very often she is said to have been the first three-decker. This cannot well be true, because the *Prince Royal* evidently had three decks; still, she was the first ship to carry anything like so many guns of any real power. She had a hundred guns, while the *Prince Royal* as originally built had only fifty-six. In rig she was interesting too. The fourth mast disappeared, and to make up for this she carried, or is shown as carrying, an extra sail at the top of each mast—'royals' on the fore and main, and a topgallant sail on the mizzen. These sails can be seen furled in Plate XI, which is taken from a contemporary engraving of the ship.

Many people refuse to believe in these royals, and

PLATE XI

THE *SOVEREIGN OF THE SEAS* (1637)

PLATE XII

MODEL OF THE DANISH *NORSKE LØVE* (1650)

certainly they were not adopted generally in the Navy for very many years. Still, it seems unreasonable to deny that such sails were sometimes carried. The Danish print of 1600 (Plate IX) showed bowlines for a main royal, and a print of the Venetian fleet dated 1619 gives royals to two ships: on the main only in one, and on both main and fore in the other. Again, an Algerine ship of 1622 is said to have had " two topgallant sails, one above another," above her main topsail, while finally—to clinch the matter—a manuscript on rigging written about 1625 says that flagstaffs " serve also for top topgallant sails." In view of all this evidence it seems that the verse from a contemporary description of the *Sovereign*—

> Whose brave Top top-top Royal nothing bars
> By day to brush the Sun, by night the Stars—

must mean something more than that her masts were unusually high.

A year after the *Sovereign of the Seas*, in 1638, the French launched a ship of almost exactly the same size, called the *Couronne*. There is no picture of this ship, but we know that she was a two-decker of seventy-two guns. The model of her in the Louvre in Paris was based on a print which really represents a French ship built in Holland twelve years earlier. For a Danish ship of about this time, the *Norske Løve* of 1634, there still exists a wonderful ivory model. This was not finished till 1654 and does not quite agree with what is known of the actual ship's measurements and guns, but it gives a very good idea of a moderate-sized man-of-war of the first half of the seventeenth century. A photograph of this model appears in Plate XII.

After about 1650 wooden models, properly built to scale, begin to be found. There is one in Amsterdam of the Dutch East Indiaman *Prins Willem* of 1649, another in Stockholm of the Swedish fifty-gun ship *Amarant*, built in 1653. The earliest-known English scale-model is also in Stockholm (Fig. 94); it was made by a

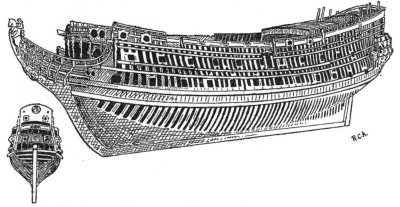

Fig. 94. ENGLISH MODEL OF 1658 IN THE STOCKHOLM NAVAL MUSEUM

Royalist shipbuilder named Sheldon who fled to Sweden in 1658, and either took the model with him or made it when he got there as a sample of his skill. In England it is doubtful if we have any model as old as this, but the *Prince* of 1670 at South Kensington is a particularly fine specimen for so early a date.

In the drawing of the *Amarant* (Fig. 95), for which we have to thank Admiral Hägg of the Swedish Navy, there is a row of reef-points in the topsails. For some reason not yet fully understood, reef-points, after appearing fairly often in pictures and seals up to the beginning of the sixteenth century, vanish altogether for more than a hundred years. They appear again, in the topsails this time, somewhere about 1660. At the

same time we begin to find ' staysails,' which were triangular sails of much the same shape as the lateen
mizzen, set on the stays of the masts and topmasts.
These begin to appear in pictures after 1658, though

Fig. 95. SWEDISH SHIP *AMARANT*, 1653
Drawn by Admiral Hägg from the model

they can be found in lists of stores a few years sooner.
Staysails were not new ; they had been used in small
craft, together with the fore-and-aft spritsail, for at
least two hundred years; it was only their use in full-
rigged ships that was new. Probably it began as a
' jury rig '—that is to say, an emergency rig after damage
by weather or battle. A letter of 1639 speaks of setting

147

a mizzen on the mainstay for this purpose, and something similar is shown in Fig. 96 from a Dutch etching of about 1653 by Zeeman, where a Dutch ship badly damaged is seen towing an English prize in an even worse state. In this case the English ship has a triangular sail beneath her mizzen-stay, while the Dutchman has either set a topsail on the stump of his

Fig. 96. JURY RIGS
About 1653

mizzen-mast or has rigged up a sail like that mentioned in the case of the *Prince Royal*—a square sail under the crojack-yard.

Zeeman, whose real name was Nooms, was one of the Dutch seventeenth-century artists to whom we owe so much. Thanks largely to them, our knowledge of the ships of the second half of that century is greater than that of any previous period. It is not that the ships themselves changed much ; it is simply that we know more about them. Models begin to be fairly common. Books on shipbuilding are found in England, France, and Holland, while a great store of other writings is preserved in manuscript. Above all, we have the drawings of the great Dutch artists, particularly the two Van de Veldes, father and son. Between them they were hard at work from about 1639 to 1701. The father was on board the Dutch fleet against the Spaniards in 1639 as official artist, and he and his son

148

were employed in the same way through the wars of the next thirty years. Somehow Charles II got them into his service in 1672 and gave them a regular salary. They combined great accuracy with speed, and thus their drawings have almost the value of photographs.

The drawing of the English yachts *Mary* and *Charlotte* from the Fodor Museum in Amsterdam (Plate XIII) is a good example of the work of the younger Van de Velde. Yachts had long been used in Holland as a comfortable way of getting about in that country of narrow and shallow waterways. They were first used in England in 1660, when the Dutch gave a yacht to Charles II on his restoration. The King was delighted with his present, saw its possibilities in deeper water, and at once ordered his own builders to try their hands at similar boats. Very soon he and the Duke of York were sailing races on the Thames and thus starting a fine sport that is still favoured with Royal patronage. The first English yacht, which was also called *Mary*, having been built in Holland had leeboards such as are seen to-day in the Thames barge, to take the place in a shallow-draught vessel of the deep keel which is necessary to let a ship beat to windward. In her English-built successors these leeboards were abandoned, and the hulls were built deeper instead.

One important feature of this period was the sudden rise of the French Navy. It had been important early in the century, but it had then collapsed and had left the Dutch, who had just crushed the last of Spain's naval power at the Battle of the Downs in 1639, to fight out with England the question of which should be the greatest naval Power in the world. In the first of these three wars the French were neutral, though part of their fleet was, as a matter of fact, attacked and captured by the English. In the second they sided with Holland, but did very little; and in the third they joined the English against the Dutch. By then they were becoming a force to be considered; a few years later they met and beat Dutch and Spaniards together in the Mediterranean, and finally in 1690 at Beachy Head they were strong enough to defeat the combined fleets of Holland and England.

Very early in this revival the French were leading the way in matters of design. In 1667 they were still buying ships from Holland and Denmark, and yet by 1672 a French-built ship, the *Superbe*, of seventy-four guns, was thought worthy of being taken as a pattern by Sir Anthony Deane, the chief designer of the English Navy. The great thing about these French ships was that they were very large and, more especially, very wide for the number of guns they carried. Such a ship as the *Superbe* would be almost as big as an English ninety-gun three-decker. This naturally made them better able to stow their provisions and to use their guns in all weathers. The same thing had been the case in 1638, when the *Couronne* of seventy-two guns was as big as the *Sovereign of the Seas* of a hundred, and it went on all through the next century; each increase in dimensions was forced on English builders by foreign models, and each time the foreigners promptly went one better again.

For a little time French ships were disfigured by an absurd mass of decoration. For instance, the *Monarque*, a three-decker, had on her stern twenty-seven wooden statues, all bigger than life size; and at one time Puget, their chief decorator, seriously claimed that the actual structure of the ship ought to be arranged to suit his ideas of ornament. Naturally, when ships such as that in Fig. 97 went to sea the captains sometimes took the opportunity to cut away part of this useless load.

Fig. 97. STERN OF FRENCH SHIP *ROYAL LOUIS*, 1668

Dutch ships were plainer. In their case the chief feature was usually a picture or carving on the upper part of the stern representing something in connexion with the ship's name. In the example given in Fig. 98 the ship is the *Utrecht,* and the arms on the stern are those of that town. From this practice comes the English word 'taffrail' for the top of a ship's stern ; *tafereel* was the Dutch for a picture. In English ships

151

the greater part of the stern-decoration consisted, about 1670, of the Royal Arms carved very large. Later on the Arms got smaller, and all sorts of figures

Fig. 98. STERN OF DUTCH SHIP *UTRECHT*
About 1670

were added above them. In Amsterdam they still have the actual carved Royal Arms from the stern of the *Royal Charles*, which they captured in the Medway in 1667.

A drawing of this ship is given here as showing a

large English ship of the middle of the century (Fig. 99). She had been built in 1655 as the *Naseby* and had been renamed at the Restoration. By comparing this drawing with that of the *Amarant* (Fig. 95), which was very like a Dutch ship, one can get a good idea of the main differences between English ships and their chief rivals.

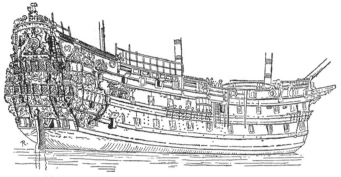

Fig. 99. ENGLISH SHIP *ROYAL CHARLES* (FORMERLY *NASEBY*)
Built in 1655

Quite apart from the shape of the stern, there were other striking differences both in hull and rigging. The quarter-galleries were entirely different, as can be seen from Figs. 100 and 101, and the upper works of Dutch ships were always clinker-built, while the English used the ordinary carvel planking everywhere. In rigging the most obvious difference was in the shape of the caps of the masts. In the early days of topmasts they had simply been lashed to the heads of the lower masts. A little later, as topmasts grew, it became desirable to be able to lower them in bad weather. This invention, by the way, is claimed by the Dutch and ascribed to the year 1570. It had certainly come into general use by the end of the sixteenth century. The top on the lower mast was supported by two 'trestle-trees' running fore and aft and two 'cross-trees' running athwartships. Between the two trestle-trees and between the head of the lower mast and the foremost cross-tree there was a square hole into which the heel of the topmast fitted. At the extreme head of the lower mast there was a 'cap,' a block of wood with a square hole in it for the end of the lower mast and a round hole for the topmast. To keep the topmast from slipping down a metal wedge

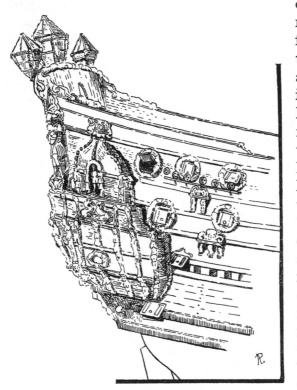

Fig. 100. ENGLISH QUARTER GALLERY
About 1670.   From a model

called a 'fid' was put through a hole in its heel just above the trestle-trees. In very early days the cap was shorter and had only a semicircular groove in its forward edge, so that the topmast still had to be lashed in place. Quite soon, perhaps from the very first, English caps were made roughly in the shape of a brick laid on its flat and pointing fore and aft. Dutch and other foreign caps took quite a different form ; they were wider than they were long and were roughly semi-circular in shape, looked at from the side, with a flat extension to go round the topmast. The reason for this was that, as Fig. 102 shows, they served also as leads for the ties which carried the lower yard, thus bringing about a return to something like the Southern calcet system shown in Fig. 70, while the English stuck to hounds beneath the top, or (later on) to blocks hung in much the same place.

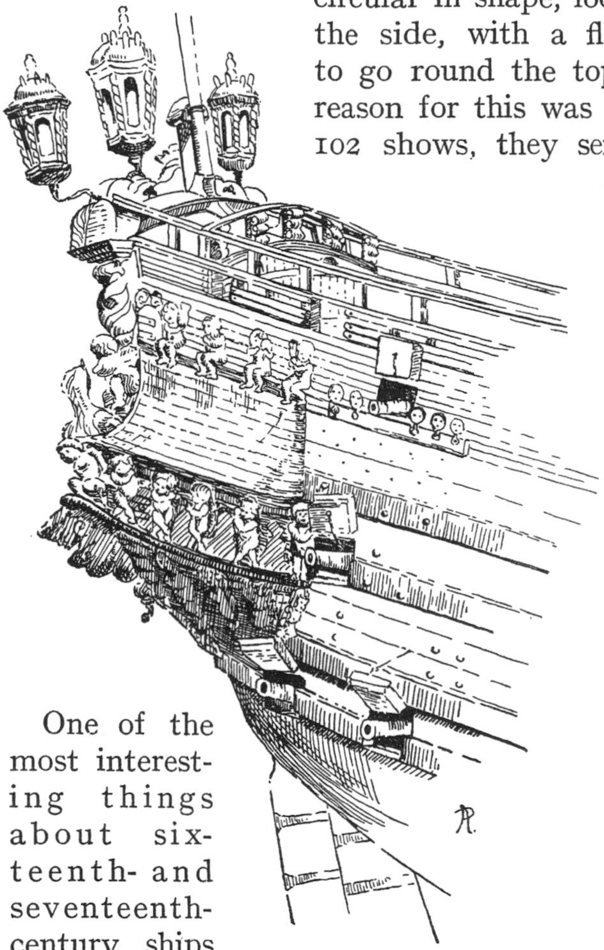

One of the most interesting things about six-teenth- and seventeenth-century ships is how they were steered.

Fig. 101. DUTCH QUARTER GALLERY
About 1670. From a model

In the early days of the stern-rudder ships were small enough for a man or several men to steer with a tiller, just as a small sailing-boat is steered to-day. Later, when the decks grew up one over another in the stern, the tiller was buried out of reach, and it was necessary to have some way of working it from above. The steering-wheel, which seems to us such an obvious con-

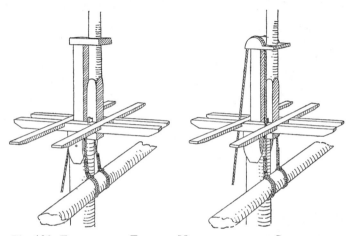

Fig. 102. English and Foreign Mastheads in the Seventeenth Century

trivance, had not yet been invented, and the tiller was controlled by means of a device called in English the ' whipstaff.' On the end of the tiller was a pin, over which fitted a ring at the end of a long thin pole. This pole passed through a pivot in the deck above the tiller, fitting loosely so that it could slide up and down as well as swing sideways. The helmsman held the upper end of the pole and by pushing or pulling he could move the tiller and thus steer the ship. Sometimes the whipstaff passed through only one deck, sometimes there was a slot for it in the deck above. In any case the helmsman was still below-deck as a general rule and depended on what he could see or hear through a small

PLATE XIII

ENGLISH YACHTS, 1678
From a drawing by W. Van de Velde the younger in the
Fodor Museum, Amsterdam

PLATE XIV

FRENCH THREE-DECKER, 1680

PLATE XV

MODEL OF A DUTCH THREE-DECKER (1685)

hatchway in the deck above him. Of course, he had a compass in front of him, and usually he would be steering by that.

The diagram in Fig. 103 is intended to show how the whipstaff worked. It shows a section across the ship at the fore end of the tiller, looking toward the stern. P is the port (left) side of the ship, S the starboard, D is the deck, C the pivot, or 'roll,' through which the whipstaff passed. A is the upper end of the whipstaff, which is connected at its lower end to the tiller B. In this position the whipstaff is upright, the tiller amidships

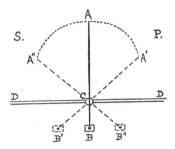

Fig. 103. DIAGRAM TO SHOW THE ACTION OF THE WHIPSTAFF

and the rudder doing nothing either way. If the whipstaff is swung over to A' and at the same time pushed downward the tiller will move over to B' on the starboard side of the ship. This will take the rudder to port, and the ship will turn to port.

This method of steering could not put the rudder over very far, and a good deal must have been done by altering the trim of the sails. When it blew hard the whipstaff had to be disconnected altogether, and steering had to be done by means of tackles on the tiller. It was an unsatisfactory contrivance in many ways, and the wheel, when it appeared, must have been a real boon.

The wars of this century were far nearer true naval warfare than any before ; in fact the first Anglo-Dutch war of 1652–54 was almost a perfect example. As a result of so much fighting with gradually improving ships there grew up an understanding of the best ships for particular purposes, and of the best way to use them. Up to 1650, or thereabouts, all the ships in a fleet, big and small, went into action in a lump. By 1653 the English fleet was ordered to fight in line ahead, one ship behind another. This was clearly the best way to employ ships whose guns fired almost entirely on the broadside, but very exact handling was required to keep station, and this had been made possible only by recent improvements in rig. Line-ahead formation had one drawback : unless a commander could know exactly how his opponent's ships were arranged there was a danger that a very small ship might find herself opposite a very powerful enemy. The only way out of this difficulty was to keep the smallest ships out of the line altogether, and to use only those which would have a fair chance of standing up to anything they might meet.

The result was that all ships of less than about fifty guns dropped out of the class considered ' fit to lie in a line.' Even so, a fifty-gun two-decker might find herself engaged with a three-decker of twice as many guns, and those heavier than her own. In the last of the Dutch wars the English used three-deckers of a hundred or ninety guns and two-deckers ranging from seventy to forty-eight guns. The Dutch had no three-deckers, but had very powerful two-deckers of eighty guns or more. The French built both types.

A two-decker was a ship with two rows of guns running the whole length of her lower and upper decks. Above these would come an interrupted row of guns on the quarterdeck and forecastle with a gap amidships, and above them again, in the biggest ships, would be a few guns on the poop. A three-decker would add to these a third complete tier of guns. Thus what was called a two-decker might have no less than four guns above one another in the stern.

Toward the end of the century the English tried to build big two-deckers, and the Dutch three-deckers. In neither case was the result a success. The English eighty-gun two-deckers proved too weak in their upper works, and the last of them were made into a sort of mongrel three-deckers, with a complete upper deck without a complete row of guns. The Dutch ninety-gun ships were three-deckers with no forecastles and with very short quarterdecks. They were too small for their guns, and only the last two or three, which were larger, were at all satisfactory.

To illustrate the changes of the seventeenth century the ship of 1594 in Fig. 91 may be compared with a French ship of about a hundred years later (Plate XIV). The straightening of the hull is very marked. In rig the most obvious changes are at either end of the ship, the fixed spritsail and the spritsail topsail on the bowsprit, and the single mizzen with a square topsail in place of the two mizzens with a lateen topsail to one of them.

For a good idea of English and Dutch ships of the end of the century one cannot do better than turn to models. The two illustrated in Plates XV and XVI are each remarkable in its way. The Dutch model, which represents one of the first of their three-deckers, built about 1685, is believed to be the only model of a Dutch three-decker in existence. The English model, the *St George* of 1701–2, is remarkable for having contemporary rigging in perfect condition. A model's rigging is delicate stuff, very liable to damage, and most models of any age, if they have been rigged at all, either have been allowed to fall into a state of utter wreck or

have been 'restored' with rigging suitable to a date
very much too late for the hull. This had happened to
the Dutch model shown here ; the rigging had been
done, very roughly, after the fashion of Napoleonic
times. It has now been removed altogether and replaced by rigging based on books and pictures of the
right date. Such modern work is better than old rigging
that does not belong to the same date as the hull, but it
is naturally nothing like so valuable as real contemporary work. The *St George* model owes its perfect
rigging to the fact that, until quite recently, it had
been kept in the same house and the same case since
it was first made. Alas ! this beautiful model, like so
many others, has now left its home and its country for
America.

The open-work, unplanked hull below the waterline is
a feature that is nearly always found in English Navy
Board models—that is to say, in the models which
were made for official use. Foreign models are usually
planked all over. Sails are not often shown, and less
often on English models than on foreigners. One must
imagine a furled sail beneath each yard. This absence
of sails makes it necessary to fix to the yards certain
ropes, such as the bowlines, which would naturally be
attached to the sails, and to show the topsail-yards
lowered right down, as they would be when the sails
were furled.

One important new fitting appears in this *St George*
model. This is the rope called the ' bobstay ' leading
from the bowsprit to a point below the figurehead. The
bowsprit had to take the direct strain of the forestay,
fore topmast-stay and fore topgallant-mast stay, and
indirectly that of the main topmast and main top-

PLATE XVI

MODEL OF THE *ST GEORGE* (1701)

gallant-mast stays as well. These strains came well out along the bowsprit, and the only thing to hold it down was the 'gammoning,' a heavy lashing between the figurehead and the stem of the ship. It seems extraordinary that it should have taken more than two hundred years before the bobstay was thought of to

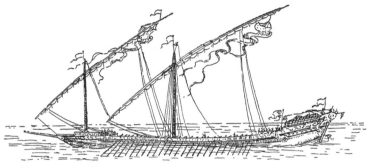

Fig. 104. FRENCH GALLEY OF ABOUT 1700

help the bowsprit in its work, but such was the case. Probably it was that early beak-heads were not suitable in shape or construction to stand the pull. Early examples of the bobstay are found in a French print of 1691, and on a Dutch model rigged in 1698.

Thanks to models and descriptions, we have a good idea of the internal arrangements of ships of the seventeenth century. The captain and officers were accommodated in the after part of the ship under the poop, quarterdeck, and half-deck. The gunner and his mates lived in the gunroom, right in the stern below the officers' quarters. Some of the inferior officers, such as the boatswain and carpenter, had cabins against the bulkheads which shut off the forecastle and the half-deck or quarterdeck from the open upper deck. The crew lived along the covered decks between the guns and slept there in hammocks. The cook-room was at first placed in the hold amidships, but was afterward shifted to the forecastle. Ammunition and stores of various kinds had their places in the hold beneath the lower deck.

Nothing has been said in this chapter about Mediterranean ships. There is very little to say. Apart from the French, whose ships have already been considered, the only important naval Powers in the Mediterranean were the Venetians and the Turks. Both of these relied more on galleys than on sailing-ships, and the galley had reached a state of such perfection in its own way that very little change was likely. The drawing in Fig. 104 shows a galley of about 1700 ; with a rather smaller foremast it might stand for one of a century earlier, and with the possible addition of a small mizzen it would not have looked out of date even in 1800. For sailing-ships the Venetians and Turks were dependent to a great extent on ships hired or taken from the Dutch and English. The Mediterranean nations had done their share when they produced the carrack in the fifteenth century ; after that nearly all progress in sailing-ships came from the North and West.

CHAPTER IX

THE SHIP OF THE LINE AND HER SATELLITES
A.D. 1700–1840

THE seventeenth century had seen the chief fighting-ship, the 'ship of the line' or 'line-of-battle ship,' reach the form in which she remained, save for a few minor improvements, until steam did away with sailing warships altogether. The next century saw the appearance of an equally definite type of smaller ship intended for scouting and for the attack and defence of commerce. This was the 'frigate' as she was in Nelson's day. In such a ship speed and seaworthiness were the important matters, and their combination in a ship which was not too large and expensive took a long time to achieve.

At one time there had been no definite gap between the ships meant for fighting in a fleet and those intended to cruise separately. Later on, when fifty guns became the least force considered suitable for a ship of the line, the classes below these were the forty-gun two-decker and the single-decked twenty-gun ship. Both of these proved unsatisfactory, and in the end the problem was solved by the introduction of the frigate in her later form, in which she was really a two-decked ship with no guns on her lower deck.

The name 'frigate,' or a similar word in other languages, had very different meanings at different times. In the sixteenth century the Mediterranean frigate was an oared vessel smaller than a galley and used mainly for dispatch-carrying. In the middle of the seventeenth century there were purely sailing frigates in the fleets of England, Holland, and France. It is difficult to say what distinguished these from other ships. Certainly the distinction was not one of size, for the *Naseby*, one of the biggest and most powerful English ships, was called a frigate. Some people think that it was a question of shape under water, others that it had something to do with the arrangement of the decks, others again that it meant a ship with less in the way of upper works than the old type. We know that Sir Christopher Wren had a " draught of an old-fashioned ship and another of the frigate fashion " given him by one of the Pett family, but these are not to be found now, and the matter remains a mystery. At any rate we first find frigates in English lists in 1645, and after that practically every ship built under the Commonwealth is so classed.

The usual story is that the *Constant Warwick*, built in 1646 by Peter Pett, was the first frigate in England, and that Pett copied her design from a French ship. As a matter of fact, the first lists in which this ship appears never call her a frigate, but do contain a *Warwick Frigate*, and this other ship seems to have come from Dunkirk, where they went in for building fast ships as privateers. This might explain the story of a French origin for the type. In any case the *Constant Warwick* was an ordinary small two-decker, quite different from the later frigate design.

The frigate of the eighteenth century seems to have grown out of a class of ships of some twenty-four to thirty-two guns built with two decks, but having only one or two guns a side on the lower deck and carrying oars there instead. The lower-deck guns were useless in any sea and were soon given up altogether, while the oar-ports were shifted to the upper deck and then disappeared. In England the first ships of the new pattern

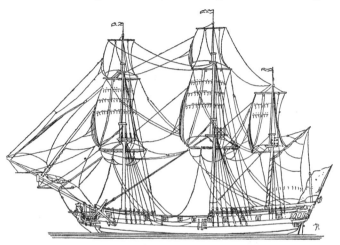

Fig. 105. FRIGATE OF 1768

were launched in 1756–57, and carried twenty-eight or thirty-two guns. France must have been a few years ahead, since a French book of 1752 mentions similar ships.

The drawing of a frigate from a Swedish book of 1768 (Fig. 105) shows two striking changes in rig. A new sail right forward had appeared very early in the eighteenth century, if not in the seventeenth. There were already two staysails on the bowsprit, the fore staysail and the fore topmast-staysail ; the new sail, the ‘ jib,’ was another triangular sail set between the fore topmast-head and a short spar, called the ‘ jib-boom,’ which was added as a prolongation of the bowsprit.

This sail was adopted officially in the English fleet in 1705, and it is safe to suppose that it must have been seen now and then for several years before that. Naturally the jib and the spritsail topsail got in one another's way,

Fig. 106. Bow of Turkish Ship
of 1760

but still they were carried together for some years. The photograph in Plate XVII from a model of the *Royal George* of 1715 shows this very well. In England the spritsail topsail was abolished for all but the largest ships in 1721 and vanished altogether soon after. Some countries kept it longer. The Spanish ship captured by Anson in the Pacific in 1743 had it, and a drawing of a Turkish ship as late as 1760 shows the top at the end of the bowsprit and the knee which would support the topmast, though the actual topmast is no longer there (Fig. 106).

This drawing shows a flag hanging beneath the jib-boom as a sign that the ship has been captured. As a matter of fact, she was carried off by some of the Christian slaves in her crew and was taken to Malta, though in the end the Knights were obliged to return her to Turkey.

The other change, in the mizzen, came in a little later than the jib. From its first introduction, for three

PLATE XVII

MODEL OF THE *ROYAL GEORGE* (1715)

THE SHIP OF THE LINE

hundred years or so, the mizzen had been a lateen. Now, a little before the middle of the eighteenth century, the part of the sail before the mast was done away with, and the mizzen assumed the shape of a gaff-sail. It is interesting to note that this half-mizzen was sometimes called a ' bonaventure ' ; this was obviously due to the tradition that that was the name for the aftermost of two mizzens. Small ships very soon lost the mizzen-yard altogether and had a real gaff mizzen, such as is seen in Fig. 105, but the bigger ships in the English Navy kept the long yard for the reason that it was a useful spar in case of damage to one of their other yards. It disappeared finally about 1800. At the battle of the Nile in 1798 one ship, Nelson's flagship *Vanguard*, had it, but by Trafalgar it was a thing of the past.

About the same time as the introduction of the jib several small changes in hulls took place. The English round-tuck stern began to be generally copied abroad, while English ships in their turn followed foreign fashion in the raising of the chainwales, or ' channels,' the pro-jecting platforms to which the shrouds of the lower masts were attached. In the latter half of the seven-teenth century the position of the channels had been one of the points where English ships differed from most others. In them the channels were below the middle-deck guns, in Dutch ships they were above those guns, and in French ships, as can be seen in Plate XVI, they were sometimes even above the upper-deck guns of a three-decker. After 1706 English ships followed the Dutch fashion. Three years earlier an order had been issued to do away with most of the useless but very ornamental carving with which English ships were covered. Heavily carved brackets gave

167

place to simple mouldings, and the elaborate wreaths round the ports (Fig. 107) that had been such a feature of seventeenth-century English ships disappeared first from the upper deck and then from the quarterdeck as well. By the end of Queen Anne's reign the trans-

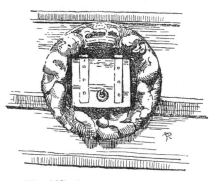

formation was complete. The seventeenth-century ship had gone and the eighteenth-century ship had arrived.

A much more important change was caused by the invention of the steering-wheel. At present it is impossible to ascribe this to a definite date or country. An

Fig. 107. PORT-WREATH, FROM A MODEL OF 1700

early piece of evidence for a wheel is found in a draught for rebuilding the English ninety-gun ship *Ossory*. This is not dated, but the ship was launched in 1711 and the draught is probably at least three years earlier, perhaps more. There is also a model at Greenwich with the date 1706 on it which has both the wheel and the pivot in the deck for the whipstaff. Another model at Greenwich, undated, but belonging to the very early years of Anne's reign, has a very interesting fitting (Fig. 108) in the shape of a two-handled windlass just where the wheel would be and connected with the tiller in the same way.

The working of the wheel was very simple. As can be seen in Fig. 109, a rope was fixed to the axle of a wheel and given several turns round it. The two ends led down through the deck and then to the two sides of the ship, abreast of the end of the tiller. Passing through two blocks there, they were made fast to either side of the tiller. By turning the wheel one end of the rope was slacked off and the other pulled in ; thus the tiller was pulled to one side and the ship was steered.

The whipstaff did not disappear altogether for some time. The *Naval Expositor* of 1750 gives it and the wheel on the same page,

Fig. 108. Steering Windlass, from an English Model of about 1705

and a Spanish manuscript of about the same date also illustrates both devices. A French naval dictionary of as late as 1765 mentions the whipstaff and not the

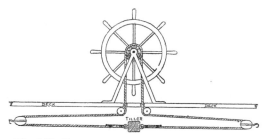

Fig. 109. Diagram to show the Action of the Steering-wheel

wheel, but this may be merely a matter of careless copying from an earlier book. Possibly foreign countries kept the whipstaff later than England. There is very little information on the matter, except that the Venetians, who were not usually very up to date with their sailing-ships, adopted the wheel officially in 1719.

Oars, which were sometimes used in early frigates, were more common in the next smaller class of ships, the ' sloops,' or ' corvettes,' as the French called them. This name ' sloop ' is even more of a puzzle than ' frigate.' At one time there was a sloop rig and a

Fig. 110. ENGLISH BRIGANTINE-RIGGED SLOOP, 1729

sloop rating, or class, and the two had nothing what-ever to do with one another. To make matters worse, a book of 1750 says that sloops " are sailed and masted as men's fancies lead them, sometimes with one mast, with two, and with three." It would be difficult to imagine a vaguer description.

Still, in the latter part of the eighteenth century, when sloops were definitely the next class below frigates, they were all very much the same in hull and were rigged in one of two ways. They were single-decked vessels carrying about eighteen guns and they had either the

170

ordinary ship-rig or that of a 'brig,' with two masts. The word 'brig' is an abbreviation of 'brigantine '— it is a mistake to look on 'brigantine' as a diminutive of 'brig.' In the longer form it came from the Mediterranean, where it meant a small lateen-rigged vessel mainly intended for rowing. Brigantines appeared in

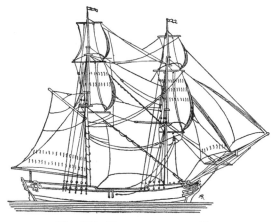

Fig. 111. BRIGANTINE OF 1768

the North toward the end of the seventeenth century, and there also they had oars, but the rig was quite different. It was two-masted, with an ordinary square-rigged foremast and a lighter but taller form of square mainsail. Very soon the mainmast exchanged this square sail for a gaff-sail with a boom at its foot—a form of sail that was called a 'brigantine sail' in some countries. Fig. 110 shows a brigantine of this type from an English engraving of 1729, and it is worth mentioning that the vessel shown is the *Drake* 'sloop.' Side by side with this type there was a true Northern two-master, the 'snow,' at first simply square-rigged on two masts, but soon having also a gaff-sail, called

the 'trysail,' set on a little mast running up close
abaft the mainmast and fixed under the maintop.
This trysail-mast was sometimes called the 'snow
mast.' Eventually the brigantine (Fig. 111) and the
snow (Fig. 112) were combined in a single type, the

Fig. 112. Snow of 1768

man-of-war brig, which had the square mainsail of the
snow and the gaff-and-boom mainsail of the brigantine
on the same mast (Fig. 113).

After the first twenty years of the eighteenth century
we hear very little about the Mediterranean galley.
The last of the wars between Venice and Turkey ended
in 1718, after a struggle in which the Turks were
opposed by squadrons belonging to Spain, Portugal,
the Pope, and the Knights of Malta, as well as the
whole navy of Venice. After this the Eastern Mediterranean had a period of comparative peace, while the
fighting in the western part between England, France,
and the reviving navy of Spain was carried on by
sailing-ships only. There were still galleys in the

Venetian fleet when Napoleon seized it in 1797, and some of the smaller Mediterranean states kept them even later, but the days of great battles between fleets of galleys were over for good.

Fig. 113. MAN-OF-WAR BRIG
About 1830

Rowing men-of-war were not altogether finished, for they survived in the Black Sea and the Baltic. The Turks built galleys, and Peter the Great, when he founded the Russian Navy in 1694, had to have galleys to meet them. Curiously enough, his pattern galley was built in Holland, but a model at Amsterdam shows that it was very similar to the usual Mediterranean galley of the time. This can be seen by comparing Fig. 114, which shows this model, with Fig. 104, which is a French Mediterranean galley of about the same date. Finding galleys useful in the Black Sea, where they were used in action as late as 1791, Peter began in 1703 to build them in large numbers for use against the Swedes in the Baltic. There the peculiar nature of

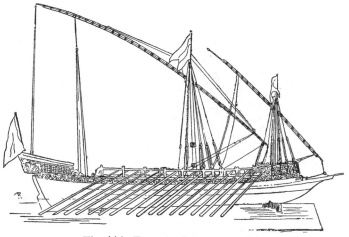

Fig. 114. RUSSIAN GALLEY OF 1694
From a model

the coast of Finland gave great advantage to shallow-draught vessels which were independent of the wind. In such a maze of rocks and islands sailing-ships were helpless, and a rowing flotilla was necessary. Both sides gradually produced a whole series of oared vessels, ranging from something very like an ordinary sailing frigate to an open boat with one big gun, and with these some important actions were fought.

As the last attempt at the combination of the galley and the sailing man-of-war these vessels are worth a little attention. The 'hemmema' which the Swedes built about the end of the eighteenth century was practically a twenty-six-gun frigate with oars in pairs between her guns. The ' turuma,' dating from about 1775, worked her oars from long outriggers like those of a galley. Her twenty-four heavy guns were below the outriggers, and an equal number of light swivel-

Fig. 115. SWEDISH UDEMA, 1780

guns above them. The ' udema ' (Fig. 115) had her nine heavy guns along the middle line, so mounted that they could be used on either side, and firing right across the outriggers. This drawing we owe to Admiral Hägg. The ' pojama ' was more like a galley, with two heavy guns at each end. She was a two-master, with a square-rigged mainmast and a gaff mizzen ; the others were three-masters with a more or less simplified ship-rig. Gun-sloops had a heavy gun at each end, gunboats one aft only. In Russia the two main types were ' shebeks ' and gunboats. The first were adaptations of the Mediterranean ' xebec,' a sailing descendant of the mediæval galley. The sketches show a Mediterranean xebec of the middle of the eighteenth century (Fig. 116) and two forms of Russian shebeks of some thirty years later (Fig. 117), and show that the lateen-rig was modified in the North, though galleys proper, even in the

Fig. 116. SPANISH XEBEC
From a drawing of 1761

Baltic, kept their lateen-rig to the last. Denmark also built gunboats in large numbers, and these proved able to meet even ships of the line in favourable conditions.

Except that they lost still more of their decoration and that their upper works got rather straighter and flatter, there was not much change in ships' hulls before the last years of the eighteenth century. One point worth mentioning is that the lower wales, the strips of

Fig. 117. RUSSIAN SHEBEKS
About 1790

very heavy planking just above the waterline, instead of being in two separate strips as before, were built up solid into one broad band. This happened somewhere about 1720. Another is that the chainwales of three-deckers moved up another deck to a position above the upper-deck guns even in English ships. The *Royal George* of 1756 was apparently the first English ship in which this was done, but it did not become the rule for some time, and the *Victory* in 1765, and even the *Royal Sovereign* in 1786, were built on the old system.

The greater part of the eighteenth century was a period of stagnation in English naval architecture. Ship-builders were pinned down to a series of 'establishments,' which fixed the chief dimensions of ships of each class, and these establishments were allowed to run too long without being revised. The result was that foreign ships, particularly French and Spanish, were built very much bigger than those of the same class in England and were thus able to carry heavier guns and to use them in worse weather. The worst class of all were the three-decked eighty-gun ships. As has been said already, the original two-decked eighties were a failure, and their three-decked successors were worse. For example, Mathews, the Commander-in-Chief in the Mediterranean, wrote as follows in 1743 : " They can scarce haul up a port; the *Chichester* hauled up but her two aftermost, but was obliged soon to lower them; as for the rest of her ports, they were caulked in when she was first fitted out, and have never been opened since, nor will they ever be, except in a Mill Pond." French and Spanish seventy-gun ships at this time were bigger than the English nineties. Again, in the Seven Years War in 1756–63 French eighty-gun two-deckers were almost as big as English hundred-gun three-deckers, while the English eighty-gun ships with three decks were very much smaller. After this war the three-decked eighties were given up, and a seventy-four-gun two-decker built nearly to the foreign standard in size became the typical English ship of the line.

In exactly the same way English frigates of the early years of the nineteenth century were outclassed by American ships of the same type. English frigates classed as thirty-eight-gun ships, but carrying really forty-nine guns, found themselves opposed by American forty-fours a good deal bigger and more strongly built and carrying fifty-four guns heavier than their own. In this case there was no advantage of skill to make up for the handicap in strength, and the result was obvious.

Plate XVIII shows an English frigate of this period, with a few small changes in rigging that are worth noting. The mizzen now has a boom at its foot as in a brigantine. In this form it was called the 'driver,' a name used originally for a sort of long, narrow, square-sail that was set on a short yard hoisted to the 'peak,' or upper end, of the old mizzen-yard. At the other end of the ship there is a little spar pointing downward from the end of the bowsprit. This was called the 'martingale-boom,' or 'dolphin-striker,' and its purpose was to act as a lead for a rope which held down the jib-boom in the same way as the bobstay held down the bowsprit. The reason for this was that another sail, the flying jib, had been introduced outside the jib, set either on a longer jib-boom or on a new spar, the flying jib-boom, which prolonged the jib-boom in the same way as that spar prolonged the bowsprit. Apparently this martingale tackle came in almost exactly a hundred years after the bobstay. The earliest picture to show a bobstay dates from 1691 and the first evidence for a dolphin-striker belongs to 1794.

This is the time of the 'French-prisoner' models of which there are so many. No doubt there are models which were made by the prisoners of the Seven Years

War and the War of American Independence, but probably nine out of ten of the examples now in existence belong to the Napoleonic Wars of 1792–1815. Most of them are made of bone, though there are wooden models as well. They are usually built on quite a small scale and have hulls which are far sharper under water than the real ships of the time. It must be remembered that they were built without the plans of the actual ships to help, and that fine lines would seem to add to their ornamental qualities. Often they have English names, but really they are practically always French ships with names added to suit the people to whom they were sold. Nearly all of these models have been rigged, and in some the original rigging is in quite good condition. Evidently the makers took care to put in everything that they had heard of as possible, for their rigging always contains many details which can best be described as fancy fittings.

At the beginning of the nineteenth century the painting of ships settled down into a standard pattern. The general thing about 1790 had been to paint the lower wales, and perhaps a bit above them, black, and to have the rest of the side a fairly dark yellow. This was by no means universal, and some ships went in for much more striking effects. For instance, at the battle of the Nile in 1798 the *Zealous* had red sides with narrow yellow stripes, and the *Minotaur* had red sides with a black stripe, while most of the other English ships were yellow with narrow black stripes. The French ships had fewer black stripes and varied between light yellow and dark red. At Trafalgar the Spanish *Santa Ana* was black all over, and the *Santissima Trinidad* was dark red with white stripes. Most of the English ships had just been repainted on Nelson's own design, yellow with black port-lids and broad black stripes between the rows of ports. Except that the yellow was soon changed to white, this chequer pattern remained the standard till the last days of sailing men-of-war and was copied in merchantmen of even later date.

Just after Trafalgar there came a change in the shape of the bows of large ships. Ever since the beginning of the seventeenth century the part of the bow above the beak-head had been cut off by a square bulkhead. The lower deck had always continued as far as the natural curve of the ship's sides, but the deck or decks above that ended off short some distance abaft the stem. As the head rose the middle deck of three-deckers became round-ended as well, but up to the end of the eighteenth century the upper deck had still the square bulkhead. From its shape and its light construction this was a very weak spot, and to allow an enemy to 'rake' you, or to fire directly into your bow or stern, was often a prelude to losing your ship.

Clearly it would be a stronger method of building if the upper part of the bow was made round like the lower part, and this is what was done. In England the change seems to have begun with the *Namur*, which was a three-decker cut down to a two-decker in 1804. As a three-decker her middle deck was round-ended and when it became the upper deck it was left round. After Trafalgar the *Victory* was repaired by the same builder who had cut down the *Namur*, and on finding that her upper-deck bulkhead had been damaged out of all proportion to the round part of the bow below it he urged the general adoption of the complete round bow. After 1811 this became the rule for all English ships.

It was not exactly a new thing, for frigates had been built in a very similar manner as far back as 1760, and the round bow had also been found in certain two-decked East Indiamen which were taken over for the Navy in 1796. Another possibility is that the capture

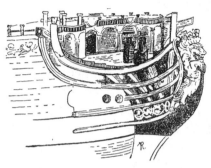

Fig. 118. SQUARE BOW
From a model of about 1730

in 1801 of a French ship that had been originally Venetian might have had something to do with it ; Venetian two-deckers had had round bows in 1780, if not earlier, and in all probability those seized by the French in 1797 had been built in the same way. Curiously enough, the ships built at Venice under the French had the ordinary square bow, and it was an incident in the capture of one of them in 1812 that led to the adoption of the round bow in the French Navy. Whatever the exact origin of the change, it was a new departure in the big ships of the more important navies and it was one that made a great difference in the appearance of ships, as can be seen from the drawings in Figs. 118 and 119.

One of the chief alterations that have recently been made in the *Victory* is the restoration of the old-fashioned bow and head in place of the round bow and raised head that had been given to her in 1813–15. Another is the opening up of the upper deck amidships. When first built, in 1765, the *Victory*, like other ships, had an open ' waist ' between the quarterdeck and forecastle with merely a light gangway on each side close to the bulwarks and above the upper-deck guns. By the time of Trafalgar she had beams across the waist, but had still only narrow gangways. In her refit the waist was planked over altogether to make a continuous deck with the quarterdeck and forecastle. This planking has now been taken away again.

Usually the gangways were quite narrow and quite lightly built ; in fact, they were very often removable. Some ships had them wider and stronger, and occasionally it was even possible to mount guns along them. This is what was done in the

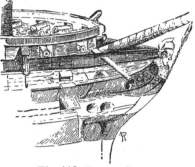

Fig. 119. ROUND BOW
From a model of about 1840

famous Spanish ship *Santissima Trinidad*. She was built in 1769 as a three-decker of 116 guns, but when rebuilt in 1795 she was given guns all along her gangways, so that she had four complete rows of ports and carried no fewer than 130 guns. Strictly speaking, she was not a four-decker, but she looked like one to her opponents and is often so called in English accounts. Frigates treated in the same way were introduced in England at the end of the Napoleonic wars as a reply to the heavy American frigates. Other countries followed, and frigates were eventually built with as many as sixty-four guns in two complete tiers, but these were called ' double-banked ' ships, not two-deckers.

After the round bow came the round stern. The weakness of the old-fashioned stern was even more serious than that of the bow. Forward, both lower and

183

middle decks of a three-decker had the protection of the main planking of the hull; it was only the upper deck that was comparatively unprotected. Aft, only the lower deck had a certain amount of protection;

Fig. 120. ROUND STERN OF THE *ASIA*, 1824
From Cooke's drawing

the rest of the ship had nothing to stop a raking fire except some glass in the stern windows and a few flimsy cabin bulkheads.

When once established custom had given way as to the shape of a ship's bow it did not take long to alter the stern as well. Seppings, who had introduced round bows, was the first to propose round sterns. This was in 1817, and in spite of much opposition the new form soon became the rule in English ships. The drawing of the stern of the *Asia* (Fig. 120) shows the new shape very well. This ship was built at Bombay in 1824 and

184

PLATE XVIII

ENGLISH FRIGATE, 1815

PLATE XIX

FRENCH MAN-OF-WAR *VALMY* (1847)

was the English flagship at the battle of Navarino in 1827, when the Turks, for the last time, were defeated by a combined fleet of other countries, this time England, France, and Russia. The French did not adopt the round stern till well on in the thirties, but Russia, then an important naval Power, took it up at once.

The stern as built by Seppings was an almost perfect semicircle, though the galleries and windows projecting from it hid its shape to some extent. Very soon a so-called elliptical stern was introduced instead ; this brought the planking round the top of the sternpost and was the final form for wooden men-of-war. The English round stern was not the first attempt to produce something better than the old-fashioned stern. Something of the sort had been tried in Denmark in the first few years of the nineteenth century. In this case the stern was made very narrow, especially in its upper part, and the shape that this gave to the sides allowed the aftermost broadside guns to fire more round toward the stern than usual, besides reducing the area of the weak part of the stern. Some of these Danish ships were taken by the English in 1807, and the advantage of their increased stern fire had been proved in action in 1811.

Ships had increased wonderfully little in length in four hundred years. The ship building at Bayonne in 1419 had been 186 feet long from stem to sternpost. This length was not exceeded till about 1700, and even in 1790 the French *Commerce de Marseille*, the biggest ship in the world, was only 211 feet long. Beyond this the sailing man-of-war never went because the old difficulty of hogging, or dropping of the ends, which we saw in ancient Egypt, had never been overcome.

Seppings introduced another novelty in a system of diagonal framing designed to prevent hogging, but even with this improvement in construction the difficulty remained. In beam there had been a slow growth from 46 feet inside the planking in 1419 to 54 feet in 1790. Finally, at the very end of the days of sailing men-of-war, there was a jump to about 60 feet. This was due to Sir William Symonds, who became Surveyor of the Navy in 1832 and was at last given a really free hand in design. There was a proposal to build a 170-gun four-decker 221 feet long and 64 feet wide, but this came to nothing. In all the smaller classes a ship of a given number of guns was very much bigger in 1800 than in 1600 or 1700, but the biggest ship considered possible had grown very little.

Plate XIX, which shows the French ship *Valmy*, of 116 guns, launched in 1847, may be taken as illustrating the last stage in the life of the full-rigged sailing warship. Such ships had had their day. Steamboats of a kind had appeared as far back as 1788 in Scotland and in America, and had become a practical means of transport before 1810. The first steam warship had been built by Fulton in America in 1814. Russia had a steamer in her navy in 1817, and the English Admiralty took up the new invention in 1822. So long as the paddle-wheel was the method of propulsion steam was of little use for actual fighting-ships, because the paddles were not only very easily damaged, but also took up a great part of the space usually given to the guns. It was only in 1836, on the invention of the screw-propeller, which was out of the way right astern and under water, that the steam line-of-battle ship became a possibility.

THE SHIP OF THE LINE

A screw sloop was built for the Royal Navy in 1843, and two years later she proved herself in every way more efficient than a paddle sloop of the same size and power. After this the screw could not be ignored. At first old ships were given engines, or ships were altered for them while building. The first English line-of-battle ship designed as a steamship was the *Agamemnon*, launched in 1852. After this the true sailing man-of-war soon disappeared, and a great epoch in naval history came to an end.

CHAPTER X

THE LAST DAYS OF THE SAILING-SHIP

THE adoption of the screw-propeller, which gave the death-blow to the sailing man-of-war, was followed almost at once by an era of great improvement in sailing merchantmen. In one way steam actually helped to make this improvement possible, because the assistance of the steam-tug for getting in and out of harbour allowed ships to be designed simply for speed and seaworthiness, without reference to the conflicting claims of handiness in narrow waters. The result was greater size, especially greater length, and in consequence greater speed.

Several other things all tending toward improvement happened within a very few years. The end of the East India Company's monopoly of trade between England and the East came in 1833, and was followed in 1842 by the opening of new Chinese ports to foreign trade, and thus by a great increase in the amount of cargo to be carried. In England the Tonnage Laws were altered in 1836 and further revised in 1854, and the old system which encouraged a narrow, deep, box-shaped vessel was replaced by one based on the real capacity to carry cargo. After this, in 1849, the Navigation Laws were repealed, and trade between England and the rest of the world was thrown open to the competition of ships of all nations. More important still, the discovery of gold in California in 1848, and in Australia in 1851, created a demand for fast ships of good size to carry the rush of emigrants and to take supplies to the new centres of population.

Up to the end of the monopoly of the East India Company English merchantmen, except for the ships belonging to that company or chartered by them, had been usually quite small ships. With the possibility of competition other owners began to build ships of about the size of the larger East Indiamen, some 1000–1500 tons. These ships were still built very much after the style of men-of-war. Five East Indiamen built on the Thames in 1796 had been bought for the Navy and completed as sixty-four-gun ships. Their dimensions, 173 feet by 43 feet, differed very little from those of two of the finest of the new ships, the *Marlborough* of 1846 and the *Blenheim* of 1848. The new vessels were about two feet longer and one or two feet narrower; otherwise, both in hulls and rigging, they were typically old-fashioned.

It was the Americans who led the way toward a faster type of ship. The first of their ' clippers,' as these fast ships came to be called, was the *Rainbow*, built at New York in 1845. Others soon followed, especially when the gold rush to California began. With the repeal of the Navigation Laws it became possible for these American ships to take part in the trade between China and England, and the enormous freights that they earned on the outward run between the Atlantic ports and San Francisco made it possible for them to cross the Pacific without cargo and then compete on equal terms with English ships. The principal trade from China was the bringing of tea, and in this speed was of the utmost importance, partly to get the first of the market and partly to lessen the bad effect which long stowage had on the tea. In this trade the Americans at first looked like having matters all their own way, for in 1850 the first of their ships to load tea for England accomplished a record passage and reached London in ninety-seven days from Hong-Kong in spite of sailing at a bad season for a fast voyage.

This ship, the *Oriental*, built at New York in 1849, may be compared with the *Blenheim*, built at Sunderland in 1848, as an illustration of the difference in type. The *Blenheim* was 175 feet long, 42 feet wide, and 29 feet deep ; the *Oriental*, 10 feet longer, was 6 feet narrower and 8 feet shallower. The difference did not stop here, for the ' lines ' of these American ships were equally revolutionary. Instead of the comparatively full bows and sterns to which sailors and shipbuilders had been accustomed for centuries, they had their ends fined down to such an extent that there was an actual hollow toward the bow and stern. This made them very much easier to drive.

English shipbuilders were quick to respond to the new challenge. Even in 1850 the *John Bunyan*, built at Aberdeen, had come home from Shanghai in ninety-nine days, and in the next year two new ships by the same builder proved themselves quite as fast as any of the Americans. In 1852 the American *Challenge* of 2000 tons was beaten by two days between the Straits of Sunda and Deal by the *Challenger* of 700 tons built on the Thames, though actually from a Chinese port to London the American did the better passage by eight days, and another American ship, the *Witch of the Wave*, sailed from Canton to Deal in this same year in ninety days, beating even the *Challenge* by fifteen days.

LAST DAYS OF THE SAILING-SHIP

All sorts of official and unofficial challenges and wagers followed. None were actually accepted, but the competition became even keener, if that were possible. It did not remain an international affair for very long, because financial troubles in the United States crippled the activities of their shipowners, and after 1860 the tea-race was left to British ships only.

In another trade, the carrying of emigrants to Australia, all the fastest ships were for some years built in America, either at Boston or at St John, New Brunswick. They were big ships of some 2000–2500 tons, and they put up records for speed that have never been surpassed by any ship driven by sails. In 1854 the *Lightning* did 436 miles in a day on her first voyage across the Atlantic, while the *Red Jacket*, which was racing her, did 413. This means that a sailing-ship was driven for a day and a night at an average speed of about 18½ knots, a speed that steamers did not reach for about another thirty years. Two years later the *James Baines* in the course of a day's run of 420 miles is said to have been travelling at one time at no less than 21 knots.

One other ' record ' of the fifties must just be mentioned. The *Dreadnought* of 1400 tons built at Newburyport, Massachusetts, is said to have made the run from Sandy Hook, outside New York, to Queenstown in Ireland in 9 days 17 hours. This is a record which was never approached by any other sailing-ship and which was, as a matter of fact, never approached by the *Dreadnought*. It has been shown that she was at least 450 miles short of Queenstown at the end of the time stated. How the story first originated is a mystery ; it is disproved quite sufficiently by the fact that her captain, when writing his memoirs, never mentioned this epoch-making passage.

The great shipping boom produced many fine ships, but none that could compare for size with the *Great Republic*, designed for the Australian trade and launched

at Boston in 1853. This ship, the biggest wooden sailing-ship ever built, was 335 feet long and 53 feet wide. Her mainmast was 131 feet long and her main-yard 120 feet. She had four masts, three of them square-rigged, and the after-mast with fore-and-aft sails. She was, in fact, what would be called nowadays a four-masted barque, or in America a jigger-rigged

Fig. 121. SIXTEENTH-CEN-TURY SHIP AND MODERN BARQUE

ship. Unfortunately, she never had a chance to show her real capacity for speed. She was very badly damaged by fire just before starting on her first voyage, and when she did at last get to sea it was with a sail-plan very much cut down in every direction.

The ordinary 'barque-rig' is three-masted, with square sails on the foremast and mainmast and fore-and-aft sails on the mizzen. It is, in fact, the rig of the sixteenth century brought up to date, and it can be traced in ships of moderate size from the first days of the three-masted ship right down to the present day (Fig. 121). In the same way the 'barquentine,' which is quite a modern rig, with square sails on the foremast and gaff-sails on the other two, may be said to be in essentials a revival of the rig of the sixteenth-century 'caravel' with her square-rigged foremast and her lateen main and mizzen (Fig. 122). In this case, however, it does not seem possible to trace the rig continuously through the intervening centuries as can be done with the barque.

Up to about the time of the *Great Republic* changes in sailing-ships were more a matter of design than of construction. The rigging was still of hemp, and the hull and spars were still of wood, though that particular ship, in view of her unusual length, was strengthened by diagonal strips of iron along her sides. In details of rigging there were a number of changes. Royals were universal, and 'skysails' above the royals had become established fittings, instead of 'captain's fancies.' Sails were now 'bent,' or attached, to iron 'jackstays' running along the upper side of the

Fig. 122. Sixteenth-cen-
tury Caravel and
Modern Barquentine

yards, instead of being bent below the yards by means of 'robands' passing round the yards. This new fashion had come in about the end of the Napoleonic wars. A little later the lower yards had been given fixed iron 'trusses' on the masts and were no longer arranged for lowering.

After this changes came with a rush. Iron ships had begun to be built as far back as 1818, and iron was well established for steamships by the middle of the nineteenth century. One of the early English clippers, the *Lord of the Isles* of 1853, was an iron ship, though iron never became popular in the China trade because of the bad effect it was supposed to have on a tea-cargo. On the other hand 'composite' ships, with iron frames and wooden planking, soon became the fashion. Iron hulls were followed by iron or steel masts and yards and by wire-rope rigging. It has been said that the English ship *Seaforth*, built in 1863, was the first ship to have steel spars and rigging. Iron must have been in use for some time before that, for the report of the International Exhibition of 1862 speaks of the use of both iron spars and iron standing rigging as having " widely spread during the last ten years," and a book of 1856 on rigging has a special section on the use of wire.

One of the most conspicuous changes in the look of ships during the gradual development of the three-masted rig had been caused by the growth of their upper sails. In a sail-plan of about 1600, one of the earliest that have been preserved, the area of the main topsail is not much more than half that of the mainsail, and the main topgallant sail is only about one-sixth of the topsail. In 1832 the main topsail was about one-tenth bigger than the mainsail, and the topgallant was more than one-third of the topsail. Looked at in another way, the mainsail formed about one-third of the total sail-area in the first case, while in the second it was less than one-sixth. The difference in appearance is shown in Fig. 123.

The enormous topsails were very heavy to handle. For warships, with their big crews, this was not such a serious matter, but for merchantmen which had to be worked with an eye to economy it was very different. The natural remedy lay in dividing the topsails into two, and this is what was done. At first, on the method invented by Captain Forbes in 1841, the yard of the lower topsail hoisted on the head of the lower mast, which had to be lengthened, while the topmast had to be put abaft the lower mast, instead of before it. This

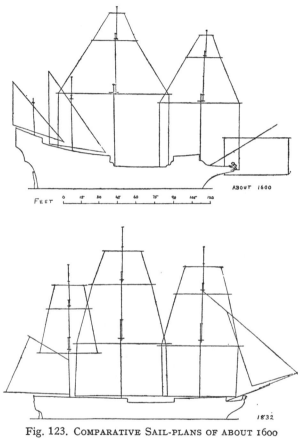

Fig. 123. COMPARATIVE SAIL-PLANS OF ABOUT 1600
AND 1832

rig was soon superseded by the modern plan introduced by Captain Howes in 1853 by which the lower topsail-yard was slung by a truss on the cap of the lower mast in the same way as the lower yard was slung on the mast itself. As originally rigged, the *Great Republic* had

195

Forbes's rig, but after the fire she came out with the newer rig invented by Howes.

The withdrawal of the Americans from the tea races caused no falling off in the keenness of these annual struggles, and each year English and Scottish builders turned out new ships in the hope of beating those of the year before. With picked crews and with captains famous for 'carrying on' these ships made wonderful passages, though none of them ever recorded such good single-day runs as the big American-built clippers of a few years earlier.

The racing was extraordinarily keen and extraordinarily level. In 1866 three ships, the *Ariel, Taeping,* and *Serica,* left Foochow in China on the same tide on May 30 and docked in London on the same tide on September 6. This was the period of composite ship-building—wooden planking on iron frames. The method had been tried occasionally for ten years or so when it was first introduced in the tea-clippers of 1863. In them it proved most successful, and it remained the almost universal build for fast ships for some ten years more before being replaced by iron and steel.

In this period of composite building the sailing-ship perhaps attained her most perfect form. Unfortunately, her prime lasted only a very short time. The possibilities of the new methods of construction and rigging had hardly been explored before the opening of the Suez Canal in the autumn of 1869 threw open the China trade to steamships and signalled the approaching death of the tea-clipper. As long as the route to the Far East lay round the Cape of Good Hope the steamer was handicapped by the fact that she had to cover a distance of more than five thousand miles between coaling-stations, and this could be done only at a very slow speed, if at all. By the Suez Canal route the longest gap was reduced to little more than two thousand miles, which made all the difference.

One of the most famous ships of the nineteenth century, the *Cutty Sark*, was launched in the very same month as the opening of the Suez Canal. She and the *Thermopylæ* of 1868 have often been described as the two fastest sailing-ships ever built. If ' fastest ' means that they were capable of the highest maximum speed the claim seems unfounded, since their best day's runs came nowhere near those of the *Lightning, James Baines, Red Jacket,* or *Donald Mackay.* That was only to be expected, because they were much smaller ships ; but it is true enough that in the matter of consistently short passages they have never been equalled.

The tea-clippers were all beautiful ships, and one of the most beautiful of all was the *Sir Lancelot*, which appears in Plate XX as an example of the highest point reached in the development of sailing-ships. Built in 1865 by Steele of Greenock, she made the fastest passage home in 1867 and 1869, and was beaten by the *Ariel* and the *Spindrift* in 1868 by only a day or less. In the last of these three races she did a record passage from Foochow to the Lizard in eighty-five days, and to her dock in London in eighty-nine days.

It was in the Australian wool-trade that competition in sailing-ships survived longest, and it was there that the *Cutty Sark* and the *Thermopylæ* made most of their reputation. In this trade the sailing-ship held her own well all through the seventies and eighties. Most of the competitors were of iron or steel, though the older composite-built ships were never outclassed. Changes in rig came

in one by one. Double topgallant sails on the same plan
as the double topsails were introduced soon after 1870.
About ten years later the rig of the *Great Republic*, a
four-masted barque, began to be fashionable, simply
because ships got bigger and the increased length de-
manded another mast. At the end of the nineteenth
century the four-masted barque-rig (Fig. 124) might

Fig. 124. A MODERN FOUR-MASTED BARQUE

have been described as the standard rig for big ships.
There were four-masted ships, square-rigged on all four
masts, and there have been a few five-masters, nearly
all barques. Some of these have reached a length of
more than 400 feet and a capacity of more than 5000
tons. The biggest of all was the French five-masted
barque *France*, built in 1913 and wrecked in 1923. She
was 430 feet long and 55¾ feet wide.

The growth in size at the end of the nineteenth
century was accompanied by a reduction in relative
sail-area and by a demand for cargo-carrying capacity
and economical working rather than extreme speed.
This brought about the disappearance of skysails and
studding-sails, and the conversion of many full-rigged
ships into barques. It also caused the adoption of

PLATE XX

Clipper-ship *Sir Lancelot* (1866)

auxiliary engines for use in calms and in narrow waters. Many a sailing-ship was lost in the Great War, and many more that are still afloat are not likely to go to sea again. At the same time the building of square-rigged ships has practically come to an end, probably for ever.

Some of the fore-and-aft rigs may live longer ; cer-

Fig. 125. A MODERN CUTTER

tainly they are in a more healthy state at present, though in most cases they are confined to inland and coasting vessels rather than real deep-sea traders. A complete account of the many forms of fore-and-aft rig, even in Europe, and of the many kinds of coasting and fishing vessels would fill a large volume; in fact this could be done with the craft of Holland alone, but a short description of a few of the chief types may be given.

Starting with one-masters, there are the spritsailed and the gaff-sailed craft, in either case with one or two triangular head-sails. Of these the sprit-rig with a triangular foresail is almost certainly the older, since it appears in a Flemish miniature as far back as 1420, or earlier, and is mentioned in writing in a German document of 1466. It has survived practically unchanged,

Fig. 126. DUTCH YACHT WITH LONG GAFF OR HALF-SPRIT
About 1780

and is still used in several kinds of small craft in Western and Northern Europe.

The gaff-sailed one-master, the 'cutter,' or sloop of the present day (Fig. 125), seems to have developed from two rather different rigs, both of which arose in Holland in the first half of the seventeenth century. In one the gaff was long and straight (Fig. 126), in the other it was very short and curved (Fig. 127). Strictly speaking, the first form was not called a gaff at all, but a half-sprit, and the sail was furled like a spritsail by brailing up without lowering the yard. No doubt this was originally a variation of the ordinary sprit-rig. The sail with the short curved gaff seems to have developed

Fig. 127. DUTCH YACHT WITH BEZAAN SAIL WITH SHORT GAFF
About 1780

from the lateen. Dutch pictures of the early part of the seventeenth century show sails which are in appearance simply lateens without a mast and with the yard acting as its own mast by having its heel stepped very far forward and its head raking well aft. This rig can just be seen in a small boat below the *Prince Royal* in Plate X. By adding a very short gaff, which at first was so small as to be little more than equivalent to the ' head-board ' of a modern racing-sail, and by reducing the rake of the mast the ' bezaan ' sail was produced, and the name, which is believed to be connected with ' mizzen,' may be taken to show that this sail was indeed developed from the lateen. With this rig the sail was lowered and stowed along the boom ; the half-sprit sail had no boom. These two forms of cutter-rig were represented in the two yachts which were given by the Dutch to Charles II on his restoration. The *Mary* had

Fig. 128. Modern Thames Barge

the half-sprit, and the *Bezan* had the rig implied by her name.

Two-masters are again either gaff-rigged or sprit-rigged, and they are further divided by the relative sizes of their two masts. Usually the sprit-rigged two-master has a big mainsail and a very small mizzen, as is seen in the Thames barge (Fig. 128) and in some Dutch craft. With the gaff-rig there is more variety, since there are types with a big mainsail and a small mizzen, with two sails of the same size, and with a big mainsail and a foresail somewhat smaller.

In England the first type is a ' yawl ' or a ' ketch,' and the last is a ' schooner.' The yawl is a gaff-rigged equivalent of the sprit-rigged barge, having a very small mizzen right in the stern. The ketch (Fig. 129) has a bigger mizzen not quite so far aft, and has developed from a square-rigged type which was originally simply a three-masted ship without the foremast. In this form it was common at the end of the seventeenth century (Fig. 130)

Fig. 129. MODERN KETCH

and later as a ' bomb vessel,' a small ship armed with a big mortar for high-angle fire. The mortar was mounted just before the mainmast, and the foremast would have been in the way of its fire. Nowadays the square mainsail has been replaced by a gaff-sail, though the square topsail is still often carried.

In the Baltic they call something very like a ketch by the old Mediterranean name of ' galeass.' The mizzen is often bigger than in the English ketch, and it is sometimes so nearly the same size as the mainsail that it is difficult to know whether the rig ought to be described in English as a ketch or a schooner.

The true two-masted schooner (Fig. 131), according

to English ideas, has a mainmast and a foremast—
that is to say, the mast nearer the stern is distinctly
the bigger. There are the usual triangular head-sails,
and there may be fore-and-aft topsails. This rig, or
something very like it, can be traced back to about

Fig. 130. ENGLISH KETCH
About 1700

1700, or a little earlier. There is a picture by the younger
Van de Velde, who died in 1707, showing two English
yachts schooner-rigged (Fig. 132), and the yacht *Transport Royal*, which was given by William III to Peter
the Great in 1697, seems to have been a schooner. Often
it is said that the first schooner was built in America in
1713 and was so called because some one at her launch
exclaimed " How she scoons ! " The story cannot be
literally true as far as rig is concerned, but it may well be
that this ship had some great improvement in hull, and
it is certainly true that the later history of the schooner-
rig is almost entirely American.

The later American schooners were, and still are,

splendid ships. The old two-masted rig has been left to the smaller specimens, and the larger vessels have been

Fig. 131. MODERN SCHOONER

built with four, five, and six masts (Fig. 133). There was indeed one seven-master, the *Thomas W. Lawson*, a

Fig. 132. SCHOONER-RIGGED YACHT
About 1700

steel ship built in 1902 and lost in 1907. One of the six-masters, the *Wyoming* of 1910, was the longest wooden sailing-ship ever built, though she had iron diagonal braces like those of the *Great Republic* ; she was 350 feet long and 50 feet wide. The biggest of the real composites, by the way, was the *Sobraon* of 1866, and she was only 317 feet long and 40 feet wide.

Many schooners have carried square topsails as well as their fore-and-aft sails. The ordinary English coasting schooner carries a square topsail on her foremast,

Fig. 133. MODERN AMERICAN SIX-MASTED SCHOONER

and sometimes a sort of temporary sail can be set beneath the lower yard. With rigs of this kind it is difficult to distinguish between a three-masted schooner and a barquentine, or between a two-masted schooner and a brigantine, which is now a vessel with a square-rigged foremast and a fore-and-aft-rigged mainmast, except by the fact that the barquentine's or brigantine's foremast is proportioned in ship fashion and has a longer lower mast and a shorter topmast than a schooner's.

Even so, there are all sorts of rigs which are difficult to classify. At least one American six-master has been rigged with all her masts exactly equal, with no gaff-sail on the foremast, and with a real square foresail and topsail both fitted on the single-stick lower mast. Whether this ship should be called a schooner or a barquentine is a difficult question.

LAST DAYS OF THE SAILING-SHIP

There are in America vessels square rigged on their two foremost masts and fore-and-aft rigged on the other two. This rig they call a four-masted barque, while the rig that would be so named on this side of the Atlantic is called in America a ' jigger-rigged ship.' The latest

Fig. 134. THE LATEST GERMAN FIVE-MASTED RIG

rig of all defies naming altogether. It is seen in recent German five-masted vessels (Fig. 134). There are gaff-sails on each mast, and the first and third masts, counting from the bow, have each four square yards as well. These set ordinary double topsails and single topgallant sails, and the lowest yard carries also a sail which is set or furled by being pulled out sideways along the yard or pulled back into a bundle lying up and down the mast.

These German five-masters like some of their larger square-rigged predecessors are fitted with auxiliary motors. Indeed the day of the pure sailing-ship of any size may be said to be past. A motor is so easy to start and easy to run that there is an ever-growing tendency in vessels with auxiliary power to use the motor more and more and the sails less and less. The actual use of sails is not likely to die entirely, any more than mankind is likely to give up walking altogether; but just as walking is no longer a usual method of travelling by land in ordinary circumstances, so sailing-ships are ceasing to be a usual method of transport by water. It may be sad, but it is certainly true.

INDEX

THE SAILING-SHIP

INDEX

THE SAILING-SHIP

A CATALOG OF SELECTED
DOVER BOOKS
IN ALL FIELDS OF INTEREST

A CATALOG OF SELECTED DOVER
BOOKS IN ALL FIELDS OF INTEREST

CONCERNING THE SPIRITUAL IN ART, Wassily Kandinsky. Pioneering work by father of abstract art. Thoughts on color theory, nature of art. Analysis of earlier masters. 12 illustrations. 80pp. of text. 5⅜ x 8½. 23411-8

ANIMALS: 1,419 Copyright-Free Illustrations of Mammals, Birds, Fish, Insects, etc., Jim Harter (ed.). Clear wood engravings present, in extremely lifelike poses, over 1,000 species of animals. One of the most extensive pictorial sourcebooks of its kind. Captions. Index. 284pp. 9 x 12. 23766-4

CELTIC ART: The Methods of Construction, George Bain. Simple geometric techniques for making Celtic interlacements, spirals, Kells-type initials, animals, humans, etc. Over 500 illustrations. 160pp. 9 x 12. (Available in U.S. only.) 22923-8

AN ATLAS OF ANATOMY FOR ARTISTS, Fritz Schider. Most thorough reference work on art anatomy in the world. Hundreds of illustrations, including selections from works by Vesalius, Leonardo, Goya, Ingres, Michelangelo, others. 593 illustrations. 192pp. 7⅛ x 10¼. 20241-0

CELTIC HAND STROKE-BY-STROKE (Irish Half-Uncial from "The Book of Kells"): An Arthur Baker Calligraphy Manual, Arthur Baker. Complete guide to creating each letter of the alphabet in distinctive Celtic manner. Covers hand position, strokes, pens, inks, paper, more. Illustrated. 48pp. 8¼ x 11. 24336-2

EASY ORIGAMI, John Montroll. Charming collection of 32 projects (hat, cup, pelican, piano, swan, many more) specially designed for the novice origami hobbyist. Clearly illustrated easy-to-follow instructions insure that even beginning papercrafters will achieve successful results. 48pp. 8¼ x 11. 27298-2

THE COMPLETE BOOK OF BIRDHOUSE CONSTRUCTION FOR WOODWORKERS, Scott D. Campbell. Detailed instructions, illustrations, tables. Also data on bird habitat and instinct patterns. Bibliography. 3 tables. 63 illustrations in 15 figures. 48pp. 5¼ x 8½. 24407-5

BLOOMINGDALE'S ILLUSTRATED 1886 CATALOG: Fashions, Dry Goods and Housewares, Bloomingdale Brothers. Famed merchants' extremely rare catalog depicting about 1,700 products: clothing, housewares, firearms, dry goods, jewelry, more. Invaluable for dating, identifying vintage items. Also, copyright-free graphics for artists, designers. Co-published with Henry Ford Museum & Greenfield Village. 160pp. 8¼ x 11. 25780-0

HISTORIC COSTUME IN PICTURES, Braun & Schneider. Over 1,450 costumed figures in clearly detailed engravings–from dawn of civilization to end of 19th century. Captions. Many folk costumes. 256pp. 8⅜ x 11¾. 23150-X

CATALOG OF DOVER BOOKS

STICKLEY CRAFTSMAN FURNITURE CATALOGS, Gustav Stickley and L. & J. G. Stickley. Beautiful, functional furniture in two authentic catalogs from 1910. 594 illustrations, including 277 photos, show settles, rockers, armchairs, reclining chairs, bookcases, desks, tables. 183pp. 6½ x 9¼. 23838-5

AMERICAN LOCOMOTIVES IN HISTORIC PHOTOGRAPHS: 1858 to 1949, Ron Ziel (ed.). A rare collection of 126 meticulously detailed official photographs, called "builder portraits," of American locomotives that majestically chronicle the rise of steam locomotive power in America. Introduction. Detailed captions. xi+129pp. 9 x 12. 27393-8

AMERICA'S LIGHTHOUSES: An Illustrated History, Francis Ross Holland, Jr. Delightfully written, profusely illustrated fact-filled survey of over 200 American lighthouses since 1716. History, anecdotes, technological advances, more. 240pp. 8 x 10¾. 25576-X

TOWARDS A NEW ARCHITECTURE, Le Corbusier. Pioneering manifesto by founder of "International School." Technical and aesthetic theories, views of industry, economics, relation of form to function, "mass-production split" and much more. Profusely illustrated. 320pp. 6⅛ x 9¼. (Available in U.S. only.) 25023-7

HOW THE OTHER HALF LIVES, Jacob Riis. Famous journalistic record, exposing poverty and degradation of New York slums around 1900, by major social reformer. 100 striking and influential photographs. 233pp. 10 x 7⅞. 22012-5

FRUIT KEY AND TWIG KEY TO TREES AND SHRUBS, William M. Harlow. One of the handiest and most widely used identification aids. Fruit key covers 120 deciduous and evergreen species; twig key 160 deciduous species. Easily used. Over 300 photographs. 126pp. 5⅜ x 8½. 20511-8

COMMON BIRD SONGS, Dr. Donald J. Borror. Songs of 60 most common U.S. birds: robins, sparrows, cardinals, bluejays, finches, more–arranged in order of increasing complexity. Up to 9 variations of songs of each species.
Cassette and manual 99911-4

ORCHIDS AS HOUSE PLANTS, Rebecca Tyson Northen. Grow cattleyas and many other kinds of orchids–in a window, in a case, or under artificial light. 63 illustrations. 148pp. 5⅜ x 8½. 23261-1

MONSTER MAZES, Dave Phillips. Masterful mazes at four levels of difficulty. Avoid deadly perils and evil creatures to find magical treasures. Solutions for all 32 exciting illustrated puzzles. 48pp. 8¼ x 11. 26005-4

MOZART'S DON GIOVANNI (DOVER OPERA LIBRETTO SERIES), Wolfgang Amadeus Mozart. Introduced and translated by Ellen H. Bleiler. Standard Italian libretto, with complete English translation. Convenient and thoroughly portable–an ideal companion for reading along with a recording or the performance itself. Introduction. List of characters. Plot summary. 121pp. 5¼ x 8½. 24944-1

TECHNICAL MANUAL AND DICTIONARY OF CLASSICAL BALLET, Gail Grant. Defines, explains, comments on steps, movements, poses and concepts. 15-page pictorial section. Basic book for student, viewer. 127pp. 5⅜ x 8½. 21843-0

THE CLARINET AND CLARINET PLAYING, David Pino. Lively, comprehensive work features suggestions about technique, musicianship, and musical interpretation, as well as guidelines for teaching, making your own reeds, and preparing for public performance. Includes an intriguing look at clarinet history. "A godsend," *The Clarinet*, Journal of the International Clarinet Society. Appendixes. 7 illus. 320pp. 5⅜ x 8½. 40270-3

HOLLYWOOD GLAMOR PORTRAITS, John Kobal (ed.). 145 photos from 1926-49. Harlow, Gable, Bogart, Bacall; 94 stars in all. Full background on photographers, technical aspects. 160pp. 8⅜ x 11¼. 23352-9

THE ANNOTATED CASEY AT THE BAT: A Collection of Ballads about the Mighty Casey/Third, Revised Edition, Martin Gardner (ed.). Amusing sequels and parodies of one of America's best-loved poems: Casey's Revenge, Why Casey Whiffed, Casey's Sister at the Bat, others. 256pp. 5⅜ x 8½. 28598-7

THE RAVEN AND OTHER FAVORITE POEMS, Edgar Allan Poe. Over 40 of the author's most memorable poems: "The Bells," "Ulalume," "Israfel," "To Helen," "The Conqueror Worm," "Eldorado," "Annabel Lee," many more. Alphabetic lists of titles and first lines. 64pp. 5³⁄₁₆ x 8¼. 26685-0

PERSONAL MEMOIRS OF U. S. GRANT, Ulysses Simpson Grant. Intelligent, deeply moving firsthand account of Civil War campaigns, considered by many the finest military memoirs ever written. Includes letters, historic photographs, maps and more. 528pp. 6⅛ x 9¼. 28587-1

ANCIENT EGYPTIAN MATERIALS AND INDUSTRIES, A. Lucas and J. Harris. Fascinating, comprehensive, thoroughly documented text describes this ancient civilization's vast resources and the processes that incorporated them in daily life, including the use of animal products, building materials, cosmetics, perfumes and incense, fibers, glazed ware, glass and its manufacture, materials used in the mummification process, and much more. 544pp. 6⅛ x 9¼. (Available in U.S. only.) 40446-3

RUSSIAN STORIES/RUSSKIE RASSKAZY: A Dual-Language Book, edited by Gleb Struve. Twelve tales by such masters as Chekhov, Tolstoy, Dostoevsky, Pushkin, others. Excellent word-for-word English translations on facing pages, plus teaching and study aids, Russian/English vocabulary, biographical/critical introductions, more. 416pp. 5⅜ x 8½. 26244-8

PHILADELPHIA THEN AND NOW: 60 Sites Photographed in the Past and Present, Kenneth Finkel and Susan Oyama. Rare photographs of City Hall, Logan Square, Independence Hall, Betsy Ross House, other landmarks juxtaposed with contemporary views. Captures changing face of historic city. Introduction. Captions. 128pp. 8¼ x 11. 25790-8

AIA ARCHITECTURAL GUIDE TO NASSAU AND SUFFOLK COUNTIES, LONG ISLAND, The American Institute of Architects, Long Island Chapter, and the Society for the Preservation of Long Island Antiquities. Comprehensive, well-researched and generously illustrated volume brings to life over three centuries of Long Island's great architectural heritage. More than 240 photographs with authoritative, extensively detailed captions. 176pp. 8¼ x 11. 26946-9

NORTH AMERICAN INDIAN LIFE: Customs and Traditions of 23 Tribes, Elsie Clews Parsons (ed.). 27 fictionalized essays by noted anthropologists examine religion, customs, government, additional facets of life among the Winnebago, Crow, Zuni, Eskimo, other tribes. 480pp. 6⅛ x 9¼. 27377-6

FRANK LLOYD WRIGHT'S DANA HOUSE, Donald Hoffmann. Pictorial essay of residential masterpiece with over 160 interior and exterior photos, plans, elevations, sketches and studies. 128pp. 9¼ x 10¾. 29120-0

THE MALE AND FEMALE FIGURE IN MOTION: 60 Classic Photographic Sequences, Eadweard Muybridge. 60 true-action photographs of men and women walking, running, climbing, bending, turning, etc., reproduced from rare 19th-century masterpiece. vi + 121pp. 9 x 12. 24745-7

1001 QUESTIONS ANSWERED ABOUT THE SEASHORE, N. J. Berrill and Jacquelyn Berrill. Queries answered about dolphins, sea snails, sponges, starfish, fishes, shore birds, many others. Covers appearance, breeding, growth, feeding, much more. 305pp. 5¼ x 8¼. 23366-9

ATTRACTING BIRDS TO YOUR YARD, William J. Weber. Easy-to-follow guide offers advice on how to attract the greatest diversity of birds: birdhouses, feeders, water and waterers, much more. 96pp. 5³⁄₁₆ x 8¼. 28927-3

MEDICINAL AND OTHER USES OF NORTH AMERICAN PLANTS: A Historical Survey with Special Reference to the Eastern Indian Tribes, Charlotte Erichsen-Brown. Chronological historical citations document 500 years of usage of plants, trees, shrubs native to eastern Canada, northeastern U.S. Also complete identifying information. 343 illustrations. 544pp. 6½ x 9¼. 25951-X

STORYBOOK MAZES, Dave Phillips. 23 stories and mazes on two-page spreads: Wizard of Oz, Treasure Island, Robin Hood, etc. Solutions. 64pp. 8¼ x 11. 23628-5

AMERICAN NEGRO SONGS: 230 Folk Songs and Spirituals, Religious and Secular, John W. Work. This authoritative study traces the African influences of songs sung and played by black Americans at work, in church, and as entertainment. The author discusses the lyric significance of such songs as "Swing Low, Sweet Chariot," "John Henry," and others and offers the words and music for 230 songs. Bibliography. Index of Song Titles. 272pp. 6½ x 9¼. 40271-1

MOVIE-STAR PORTRAITS OF THE FORTIES, John Kobal (ed.). 163 glamor, studio photos of 106 stars of the 1940s: Rita Hayworth, Ava Gardner, Marlon Brando, Clark Gable, many more. 176pp. 8⅜ x 11¼. 23546-7

BENCHLEY LOST AND FOUND, Robert Benchley. Finest humor from early 30s, about pet peeves, child psychologists, post office and others. Mostly unavailable elsewhere. 73 illustrations by Peter Arno and others. 183pp. 5⅜ x 8½. 22410-4

YEKL and THE IMPORTED BRIDEGROOM AND OTHER STORIES OF YIDDISH NEW YORK, Abraham Cahan. Film Hester Street based on *Yekl* (1896). Novel, other stories among first about Jewish immigrants on N.Y.'s East Side. 240pp. 5⅜ x 8½. 22427-9

SELECTED POEMS, Walt Whitman. Generous sampling from *Leaves of Grass*. Twenty-four poems include "I Hear America Singing," "Song of the Open Road," "I Sing the Body Electric," "When Lilacs Last in the Dooryard Bloom'd," "O Captain! My Captain!"–all reprinted from an authoritative edition. Lists of titles and first lines. 128pp. 5³⁄₁₆ x 8¼. 26878-0

THE BEST TALES OF HOFFMANN, E. T. A. Hoffmann. 10 of Hoffmann's most important stories: "Nutcracker and the King of Mice," "The Golden Flowerpot," etc. 458pp. 5⅜ x 8½. 21793-0

FROM FETISH TO GOD IN ANCIENT EGYPT, E. A. Wallis Budge. Rich detailed survey of Egyptian conception of "God" and gods, magic, cult of animals, Osiris, more. Also, superb English translations of hymns and legends. 240 illustrations. 545pp. 5⅜ x 8½. 25803-3

FRENCH STORIES/CONTES FRANÇAIS: A Dual-Language Book, Wallace Fowlie. Ten stories by French masters, Voltaire to Camus: "Micromegas" by Voltaire; "The Atheist's Mass" by Balzac; "Minuet" by de Maupassant; "The Guest" by Camus, six more. Excellent English translations on facing pages. Also French-English vocabulary list, exercises, more. 352pp. 5⅜ x 8½. 26443-2

CHICAGO AT THE TURN OF THE CENTURY IN PHOTOGRAPHS: 122 Historic Views from the Collections of the Chicago Historical Society, Larry A. Viskochil. Rare large-format prints offer detailed views of City Hall, State Street, the Loop, Hull House, Union Station, many other landmarks, circa 1904-1913. Introduction. Captions. Maps. 144pp. 9⅜ x 12¼. 24656-6

OLD BROOKLYN IN EARLY PHOTOGRAPHS, 1865-1929, William Lee Younger. Luna Park, Gravesend race track, construction of Grand Army Plaza, moving of Hotel Brighton, etc. 157 previously unpublished photographs. 165pp. 8⅞ x 11¾. 23587-4

THE MYTHS OF THE NORTH AMERICAN INDIANS, Lewis Spence. Rich anthology of the myths and legends of the Algonquins, Iroquois, Pawnees and Sioux, prefaced by an extensive historical and ethnological commentary. 36 illustrations. 480pp. 5⅜ x 8½. 25967-6

AN ENCYCLOPEDIA OF BATTLES: Accounts of Over 1,560 Battles from 1479 B.C. to the Present, David Eggenberger. Essential details of every major battle in recorded history from the first battle of Megiddo in 1479 B.C. to Grenada in 1984. List of Battle Maps. New Appendix covering the years 1967-1984. Index. 99 illustrations. 544pp. 6½ x 9¼. 24913-1

SAILING ALONE AROUND THE WORLD, Captain Joshua Slocum. First man to sail around the world, alone, in small boat. One of great feats of seamanship told in delightful manner. 67 illustrations. 294pp. 5⅜ x 8½. 20326-3

ANARCHISM AND OTHER ESSAYS, Emma Goldman. Powerful, penetrating, prophetic essays on direct action, role of minorities, prison reform, puritan hypocrisy, violence, etc. 271pp. 5⅜ x 8½. 22484-8

MYTHS OF THE HINDUS AND BUDDHISTS, Ananda K. Coomaraswamy and Sister Nivedita. Great stories of the epics; deeds of Krishna, Shiva, taken from puranas, Vedas, folk tales; etc. 32 illustrations. 400pp. 5⅜ x 8½. 21759-0

THE TRAUMA OF BIRTH, Otto Rank. Rank's controversial thesis that anxiety neurosis is caused by profound psychological trauma which occurs at birth. 256pp. 5⅜ x 8½. 27974-X

A THEOLOGICO-POLITICAL TREATISE, Benedict Spinoza. Also contains unfinished Political Treatise. Great classic on religious liberty, theory of government on common consent. R. Elwes translation. Total of 421pp. 5⅜ x 8½. 20249-6

MY BONDAGE AND MY FREEDOM, Frederick Douglass. Born a slave, Douglass became outspoken force in antislavery movement. The best of Douglass' autobiographies. Graphic description of slave life. 464pp. 5⅜ x 8½. 22457-0

FOLLOWING THE EQUATOR: A Journey Around the World, Mark Twain. Fascinating humorous account of 1897 voyage to Hawaii, Australia, India, New Zealand, etc. Ironic, bemused reports on peoples, customs, climate, flora and fauna, politics, much more. 197 illustrations. 720pp. 5⅜ x 8½. 26113-1

THE PEOPLE CALLED SHAKERS, Edward D. Andrews. Definitive study of Shakers: origins, beliefs, practices, dances, social organization, furniture and crafts, etc. 33 illustrations. 351pp. 5⅜ x 8½. 21081-2

THE MYTHS OF GREECE AND ROME, H. A. Guerber. A classic of mythology, generously illustrated, long prized for its simple, graphic, accurate retelling of the principal myths of Greece and Rome, and for its commentary on their origins and significance. With 64 illustrations by Michelangelo, Raphael, Titian, Rubens, Canova, Bernini and others. 480pp. 5⅜ x 8½. 27584-1

PSYCHOLOGY OF MUSIC, Carl E. Seashore. Classic work discusses music as a medium from psychological viewpoint. Clear treatment of physical acoustics, auditory apparatus, sound perception, development of musical skills, nature of musical feeling, host of other topics. 88 figures. 408pp. 5⅜ x 8½. 21851-1

THE PHILOSOPHY OF HISTORY, Georg W. Hegel. Great classic of Western thought develops concept that history is not chance but rational process, the evolution of freedom. 457pp. 5⅜ x 8½. 20112-0

THE BOOK OF TEA, Kakuzo Okakura. Minor classic of the Orient: entertaining, charming explanation, interpretation of traditional Japanese culture in terms of tea ceremony. 94pp. 5⅜ x 8½. 20070-1

LIFE IN ANCIENT EGYPT, Adolf Erman. Fullest, most thorough, detailed older account with much not in more recent books, domestic life, religion, magic, medicine, commerce, much more. Many illustrations reproduce tomb paintings, carvings, hieroglyphs, etc. 597pp. 5⅜ x 8½. 22632-8

SUNDIALS, Their Theory and Construction, Albert Waugh. Far and away the best, most thorough coverage of ideas, mathematics concerned, types, construction, adjusting anywhere. Simple, nontechnical treatment allows even children to build several of these dials. Over 100 illustrations. 230pp. 5⅜ x 8½. 22947-5

THEORETICAL HYDRODYNAMICS, L. M. Milne-Thomson. Classic exposition of the mathematical theory of fluid motion, applicable to both hydrodynamics and aerodynamics. Over 600 exercises. 768pp. 6⅛ x 9¼. 68970-0

SONGS OF EXPERIENCE: Facsimile Reproduction with 26 Plates in Full Color, William Blake. 26 full-color plates from a rare 1826 edition. Includes "The Tyger," "London," "Holy Thursday," and other poems. Printed text of poems. 48pp. 5¼ x 7. 24636-1

OLD-TIME VIGNETTES IN FULL COLOR, Carol Belanger Grafton (ed.). Over 390 charming, often sentimental illustrations, selected from archives of Victorian graphics—pretty women posing, children playing, food, flowers, kittens and puppies, smiling cherubs, birds and butterflies, much more. All copyright-free. 48pp. 9¼ x 12¼. 27269-9

PERSPECTIVE FOR ARTISTS, Rex Vicat Cole. Depth, perspective of sky and sea, shadows, much more, not usually covered. 391 diagrams, 81 reproductions of drawings and paintings. 279pp. 5⅜ x 8½. 22487-2

DRAWING THE LIVING FIGURE, Joseph Sheppard. Innovative approach to artistic anatomy focuses on specifics of surface anatomy, rather than muscles and bones. Over 170 drawings of live models in front, back and side views, and in widely varying poses. Accompanying diagrams. 177 illustrations. Introduction. Index. 144pp. 8⅜ x11¼. 26723-7

GOTHIC AND OLD ENGLISH ALPHABETS: 100 Complete Fonts, Dan X. Solo. Add power, elegance to posters, signs, other graphics with 100 stunning copyright-free alphabets: Blackstone, Dolbey, Germania, 97 more–including many lower-case, numerals, punctuation marks. 104pp. 8⅛ x 11. 24695-7

HOW TO DO BEADWORK, Mary White. Fundamental book on craft from simple projects to five-bead chains and woven works. 106 illustrations. 142pp. 5⅜ x 8. 20697-1

THE BOOK OF WOOD CARVING, Charles Marshall Sayers. Finest book for beginners discusses fundamentals and offers 34 designs. "Absolutely first rate . . . well thought out and well executed."–E. J. Tangerman. 118pp. 7¾ x 10⅝. 23654-4

ILLUSTRATED CATALOG OF CIVIL WAR MILITARY GOODS: Union Army Weapons, Insignia, Uniform Accessories, and Other Equipment, Schuyler, Hartley, and Graham. Rare, profusely illustrated 1846 catalog includes Union Army uniform and dress regulations, arms and ammunition, coats, insignia, flags, swords, rifles, etc. 226 illustrations. 160pp. 9 x 12. 24939-5

WOMEN'S FASHIONS OF THE EARLY 1900s: An Unabridged Republication of "New York Fashions, 1909," National Cloak & Suit Co. Rare catalog of mail-order fashions documents women's and children's clothing styles shortly after the turn of the century. Captions offer full descriptions, prices. Invaluable resource for fashion, costume historians. Approximately 725 illustrations. 128pp. 8⅜ x 11¼. 27276-1

THE 1912 AND 1915 GUSTAV STICKLEY FURNITURE CATALOGS, Gustav Stickley. With over 200 detailed illustrations and descriptions, these two catalogs are essential reading and reference materials and identification guides for Stickley furniture. Captions cite materials, dimensions and prices. 112pp. 6½ x 9¼. 26676-1

EARLY AMERICAN LOCOMOTIVES, John H. White, Jr. Finest locomotive engravings from early 19th century: historical (1804–74), main-line (after 1870), special, foreign, etc. 147 plates. 142pp. 11⅜ x 8¼. 22772-3

THE TALL SHIPS OF TODAY IN PHOTOGRAPHS, Frank O. Braynard. Lavishly illustrated tribute to nearly 100 majestic contemporary sailing vessels: Amerigo Vespucci, Clearwater, Constitution, Eagle, Mayflower, Sea Cloud, Victory, many more. Authoritative captions provide statistics, background on each ship. 190 black-and-white photographs and illustrations. Introduction. 128pp. 8⅞ x 11¾. 27163-3

CATALOG OF DOVER BOOKS

LITTLE BOOK OF EARLY AMERICAN CRAFTS AND TRADES, Peter Stockham (ed.). 1807 children's book explains crafts and trades: baker, hatter, cooper, potter, and many others. 23 copperplate illustrations. 140pp. 4⅝ x 6. 23336-7

VICTORIAN FASHIONS AND COSTUMES FROM HARPER'S BAZAR, 1867–1898, Stella Blum (ed.). Day costumes, evening wear, sports clothes, shoes, hats, other accessories in over 1,000 detailed engravings. 320pp. 9⅜ x 12¼. 22990-4

GUSTAV STICKLEY, THE CRAFTSMAN, Mary Ann Smith. Superb study surveys broad scope of Stickley's achievement, especially in architecture. Design philosophy, rise and fall of the Craftsman empire, descriptions and floor plans for many Craftsman houses, more. 86 black-and-white halftones. 31 line illustrations. Introduction 208pp. 6½ x 9¼. 27210-9

THE LONG ISLAND RAIL ROAD IN EARLY PHOTOGRAPHS, Ron Ziel. Over 220 rare photos, informative text document origin (1844) and development of rail service on Long Island. Vintage views of early trains, locomotives, stations, passengers, crews, much more. Captions. 8⅞ x 11¾. 26301-0

VOYAGE OF THE LIBERDADE, Joshua Slocum. Great 19th-century mariner's thrilling, first-hand account of the wreck of his ship off South America, the 35-foot boat he built from the wreckage, and its remarkable voyage home. 128pp. 5⅜ x 8½. 40022-0

TEN BOOKS ON ARCHITECTURE, Vitruvius. The most important book ever written on architecture. Early Roman aesthetics, technology, classical orders, site selection, all other aspects. Morgan translation. 331pp. 5⅜ x 8½. 20645-9

THE HUMAN FIGURE IN MOTION, Eadweard Muybridge. More than 4,500 stopped-action photos, in action series, showing undraped men, women, children jumping, lying down, throwing, sitting, wrestling, carrying, etc. 390pp. 7⅞ x 10⅝. 20204-6 Clothbd.

TREES OF THE EASTERN AND CENTRAL UNITED STATES AND CANADA, William M. Harlow. Best one-volume guide to 140 trees. Full descriptions, woodlore, range, etc. Over 600 illustrations. Handy size. 288pp. 4½ x 6⅜. 20395-6

SONGS OF WESTERN BIRDS, Dr. Donald J. Borror. Complete song and call repertoire of 60 western species, including flycatchers, juncoes, cactus wrens, many more–includes fully illustrated booklet. Cassette and manual 99913-0

GROWING AND USING HERBS AND SPICES, Milo Miloradovich. Versatile handbook provides all the information needed for cultivation and use of all the herbs and spices available in North America. 4 illustrations. Index. Glossary. 236pp. 5⅜ x 8½. 25058-X

BIG BOOK OF MAZES AND LABYRINTHS, Walter Shepherd. 50 mazes and labyrinths in all–classical, solid, ripple, and more–in one great volume. Perfect inexpensive puzzler for clever youngsters. Full solutions. 112pp. 8⅛ x 11. 22951-3

CATALOG OF DOVER BOOKS

PIANO TUNING, J. Cree Fischer. Clearest, best book for beginner, amateur. Simple repairs, raising dropped notes, tuning by easy method of flattened fifths. No previous skills needed. 4 illustrations. 201pp. 5⅜ x 8½. 23267-0

HINTS TO SINGERS, Lillian Nordica. Selecting the right teacher, developing confidence, overcoming stage fright, and many other important skills receive thoughtful discussion in this indispensible guide, written by a world-famous diva of four decades' experience. 96pp. 5⅜ x 8½. 40094-8

THE COMPLETE NONSENSE OF EDWARD LEAR, Edward Lear. All nonsense limericks, zany alphabets, Owl and Pussycat, songs, nonsense botany, etc., illustrated by Lear. Total of 320pp. 5⅜ x 8½. (Available in U.S. only.) 20167-8

VICTORIAN PARLOUR POETRY: An Annotated Anthology, Michael R. Turner. 117 gems by Longfellow, Tennyson, Browning, many lesser-known poets. "The Village Blacksmith," "Curfew Must Not Ring Tonight," "Only a Baby Small," dozens more, often difficult to find elsewhere. Index of poets, titles, first lines. xxiii + 325pp. 5⅜ x 8¼. 27044-0

DUBLINERS, James Joyce. Fifteen stories offer vivid, tightly focused observations of the lives of Dublin's poorer classes. At least one, "The Dead," is considered a masterpiece. Reprinted complete and unabridged from standard edition. 160pp. 5³⁄₁₆ x 8¼. 26870-5

GREAT WEIRD TALES: 14 Stories by Lovecraft, Blackwood, Machen and Others, S. T. Joshi (ed.). 14 spellbinding tales, including "The Sin Eater," by Fiona McLeod, "The Eye Above the Mantel," by Frank Belknap Long, as well as renowned works by R. H. Barlow, Lord Dunsany, Arthur Machen, W. C. Morrow and eight other masters of the genre. 256pp. 5⅜ x 8½. (Available in U.S. only.) 40436-6

THE BOOK OF THE SACRED MAGIC OF ABRAMELIN THE MAGE, translated by S. MacGregor Mathers. Medieval manuscript of ceremonial magic. Basic document in Aleister Crowley, Golden Dawn groups. 268pp. 5⅜ x 8½. 23211-5

NEW RUSSIAN-ENGLISH AND ENGLISH-RUSSIAN DICTIONARY, M. A. O'Brien. This is a remarkably handy Russian dictionary, containing a surprising amount of information, including over 70,000 entries. 366pp. 4½ x 6¼. 20208-9

HISTORIC HOMES OF THE AMERICAN PRESIDENTS, Second, Revised Edition, Irvin Haas. A traveler's guide to American Presidential homes, most open to the public, depicting and describing homes occupied by every American President from George Washington to George Bush. With visiting hours, admission charges, travel routes. 175 photographs. Index. 160pp. 8¼ x 11. 26751-2

NEW YORK IN THE FORTIES, Andreas Feininger. 162 brilliant photographs by the well-known photographer, formerly with *Life* magazine. Commuters, shoppers, Times Square at night, much else from city at its peak. Captions by John von Hartz. 181pp. 9¼ x 10¾. 23585-8

INDIAN SIGN LANGUAGE, William Tomkins. Over 525 signs developed by Sioux and other tribes. Written instructions and diagrams. Also 290 pictographs. 111pp. 6⅛ x 9¼. 22029-X

CATALOG OF DOVER BOOKS

ANATOMY: A Complete Guide for Artists, Joseph Sheppard. A master of figure drawing shows artists how to render human anatomy convincingly. Over 460 illustrations. 224pp. 8⅜ x 11¼. 27279-6

MEDIEVAL CALLIGRAPHY: Its History and Technique, Marc Drogin. Spirited history, comprehensive instruction manual covers 13 styles (ca. 4th century through 15th). Excellent photographs; directions for duplicating medieval techniques with modern tools. 224pp. 8⅜ x 11¼. 26142-5

DRIED FLOWERS: How to Prepare Them, Sarah Whitlock and Martha Rankin. Complete instructions on how to use silica gel, meal and borax, perlite aggregate, sand and borax, glycerine and water to create attractive permanent flower arrangements. 12 illustrations. 32pp. 5⅜ x 8½. 21802-3

EASY-TO-MAKE BIRD FEEDERS FOR WOODWORKERS, Scott D. Campbell. Detailed, simple-to-use guide for designing, constructing, caring for and using feeders. Text, illustrations for 12 classic and contemporary designs. 96pp. 5⅜ x 8½.
25847-5

SCOTTISH WONDER TALES FROM MYTH AND LEGEND, Donald A. Mackenzie. 16 lively tales tell of giants rumbling down mountainsides, of a magic wand that turns stone pillars into warriors, of gods and goddesses, evil hags, powerful forces and more. 240pp. 5⅜ x 8½. 29677-6

THE HISTORY OF UNDERCLOTHES, C. Willett Cunnington and Phyllis Cunnington. Fascinating, well-documented survey covering six centuries of English undergarments, enhanced with over 100 illustrations: 12th-century laced-up bodice, footed long drawers (1795), 19th-century bustles, 19th-century corsets for men, Victorian "bust improvers," much more. 272pp. 5⅜ x 8¼. 27124-2

ARTS AND CRAFTS FURNITURE: The Complete Brooks Catalog of 1912, Brooks Manufacturing Co. Photos and detailed descriptions of more than 150 very collectible furniture designs from the Arts and Crafts movement depict davenports, settees, buffets, desks, tables, chairs, bedsteads, dressers and more, all built of solid, quarter-sawed oak. Invaluable for students and enthusiasts of antiques, Americana and the decorative arts. 80pp. 6½ x 9¼. 27471-3

WILBUR AND ORVILLE: A Biography of the Wright Brothers, Fred Howard. Definitive, crisply written study tells the full story of the brothers' lives and work. A vividly written biography, unparalleled in scope and color, that also captures the spirit of an extraordinary era. 560pp. 6⅛ x 9¼. 40297-5

THE ARTS OF THE SAILOR: Knotting, Splicing and Ropework, Hervey Garrett Smith. Indispensable shipboard reference covers tools, basic knots and useful hitches; handsewing and canvas work, more. Over 100 illustrations. Delightful reading for sea lovers. 256pp. 5⅜ x 8½. 26440-8

FRANK LLOYD WRIGHT'S FALLINGWATER: The House and Its History, Second, Revised Edition, Donald Hoffmann. A total revision–both in text and illustrations–of the standard document on Fallingwater, the boldest, most personal architectural statement of Wright's mature years, updated with valuable new material from the recently opened Frank Lloyd Wright Archives. "Fascinating"–*The New York Times*. 116 illustrations. 128pp. 9¼ x 10¾. 27430-6

CATALOG OF DOVER BOOKS

PHOTOGRAPHIC SKETCHBOOK OF THE CIVIL WAR, Alexander Gardner. 100 photos taken on field during the Civil War. Famous shots of Manassas Harper's Ferry, Lincoln, Richmond, slave pens, etc. 244pp. 10⅝ x 8¼. 22731-6

FIVE ACRES AND INDEPENDENCE, Maurice G. Kains. Great back to the land classic explains basics of self-sufficient farming. The one book to get. 95 illustrations. 397pp. 5⅜ x 8½. 20974-1

SONGS OF EASTERN BIRDS, Dr. Donald J. Borror. Songs and calls of 60 species most common to eastern U.S.: warblers, woodpeckers, flycatchers, thrushes, larks, many more in high-quality recording. Cassette and manual 99912-2

A MODERN HERBAL, Margaret Grieve. Much the fullest, most exact, most useful compilation of herbal material. Gigantic alphabetical encyclopedia, from aconite to zedoary, gives botanical information, medical properties, folklore, economic uses, much else. Indispensable to serious reader. 161 illustrations. 888pp. 6½ x 9¼. 2-vol. set. (Available in U.S. only.) Vol. I: 22798-7
Vol. II: 22799-5

HIDDEN TREASURE MAZE BOOK, Dave Phillips. Solve 34 challenging mazes accompanied by heroic tales of adventure. Evil dragons, people-eating plants, blood-thirsty giants, many more dangerous adversaries lurk at every twist and turn. 34 mazes, stories, solutions. 48pp. 8¼ x 11. 24566-7

LETTERS OF W. A. MOZART, Wolfgang A. Mozart. Remarkable letters show bawdy wit, humor, imagination, musical insights, contemporary musical world; includes some letters from Leopold Mozart. 276pp. 5⅜ x 8½. 22859-2

BASIC PRINCIPLES OF CLASSICAL BALLET, Agrippina Vaganova. Great Russian theoretician, teacher explains methods for teaching classical ballet. 118 illustrations. 175pp. 5⅜ x 8½. 22036-2

THE JUMPING FROG, Mark Twain. Revenge edition. The original story of The Celebrated Jumping Frog of Calaveras County, a hapless French translation, and Twain's hilarious "retranslation" from the French. 12 illustrations. 66pp. 5⅜ x 8½. 22686-7

BEST REMEMBERED POEMS, Martin Gardner (ed.). The 126 poems in this superb collection of 19th- and 20th-century British and American verse range from Shelley's "To a Skylark" to the impassioned "Renascence" of Edna St. Vincent Millay and to Edward Lear's whimsical "The Owl and the Pussycat." 224pp. 5⅜ x 8½. 27165-X

COMPLETE SONNETS, William Shakespeare. Over 150 exquisite poems deal with love, friendship, the tyranny of time, beauty's evanescence, death and other themes in language of remarkable power, precision and beauty. Glossary of archaic terms. 80pp. 5³⁄₁₆ x 8¼. 26686-9

THE BATTLES THAT CHANGED HISTORY, Fletcher Pratt. Eminent historian profiles 16 crucial conflicts, ancient to modern, that changed the course of civilization. 352pp. 5⅜ x 8½. 41129-X

CATALOG OF DOVER BOOKS

THE WIT AND HUMOR OF OSCAR WILDE, Alvin Redman (ed.). More than 1,000 ripostes, paradoxes, wisecracks: Work is the curse of the drinking classes; I can resist everything except temptation; etc. 258pp. 5⅜ x 8½. 20602-5

SHAKESPEARE LEXICON AND QUOTATION DICTIONARY, Alexander Schmidt. Full definitions, locations, shades of meaning in every word in plays and poems. More than 50,000 exact quotations. 1,485pp. 6½ x 9¼. 2-vol. set.
Vol. 1: 22726-X
Vol. 2: 22727-8

SELECTED POEMS, Emily Dickinson. Over 100 best-known, best-loved poems by one of America's foremost poets, reprinted from authoritative early editions. No comparable edition at this price. Index of first lines. 64pp. 5³⁄₁₆ x 8¼. 26466-1

THE INSIDIOUS DR. FU-MANCHU, Sax Rohmer. The first of the popular mystery series introduces a pair of English detectives to their archnemesis, the diabolical Dr. Fu-Manchu. Flavorful atmosphere, fast-paced action, and colorful characters enliven this classic of the genre. 208pp. 5³⁄₁₆ x 8¼. 29898-1

THE MALLEUS MALEFICARUM OF KRAMER AND SPRENGER, translated by Montague Summers. Full text of most important witchhunter's "bible," used by both Catholics and Protestants. 278pp. 6⅝ x 10. 22802-9

SPANISH STORIES/CUENTOS ESPAÑOLES: A Dual-Language Book, Angel Flores (ed.). Unique format offers 13 great stories in Spanish by Cervantes, Borges, others. Faithful English translations on facing pages. 352pp. 5⅜ x 8½. 25399-6

GARDEN CITY, LONG ISLAND, IN EARLY PHOTOGRAPHS, 1869–1919, Mildred H. Smith. Handsome treasury of 118 vintage pictures, accompanied by carefully researched captions, document the Garden City Hotel fire (1899), the Vanderbilt Cup Race (1908), the first airmail flight departing from the Nassau Boulevard Aerodrome (1911), and much more. 96pp. 8⅞ x 11¾. 40669-5

OLD QUEENS, N.Y., IN EARLY PHOTOGRAPHS, Vincent F. Seyfried and William Asadorian. Over 160 rare photographs of Maspeth, Jamaica, Jackson Heights, and other areas. Vintage views of DeWitt Clinton mansion, 1939 World's Fair and more. Captions. 192pp. 8⅞ x 11. 26358-4

CAPTURED BY THE INDIANS: 15 Firsthand Accounts, 1750-1870, Frederick Drimmer. Astounding true historical accounts of grisly torture, bloody conflicts, relentless pursuits, miraculous escapes and more, by people who lived to tell the tale. 384pp. 5⅜ x 8½. 24901-8

THE WORLD'S GREAT SPEECHES (Fourth Enlarged Edition), Lewis Copeland, Lawrence W. Lamm, and Stephen J. McKenna. Nearly 300 speeches provide public speakers with a wealth of updated quotes and inspiration–from Pericles' funeral oration and William Jennings Bryan's "Cross of Gold Speech" to Malcolm X's powerful words on the Black Revolution and Earl of Spenser's tribute to his sister, Diana, Princess of Wales. 944pp. 5⅜ x 8⅜. 40903-1

THE BOOK OF THE SWORD, Sir Richard F. Burton. Great Victorian scholar/adventurer's eloquent, erudite history of the "queen of weapons"–from prehistory to early Roman Empire. Evolution and development of early swords, variations (sabre, broadsword, cutlass, scimitar, etc.), much more. 336pp. 6⅛ x 9¼. 25434-8

CATALOG OF DOVER BOOKS

AUTOBIOGRAPHY: The Story of My Experiments with Truth, Mohandas K. Gandhi. Boyhood, legal studies, purification, the growth of the Satyagraha (nonviolent protest) movement. Critical, inspiring work of the man responsible for the freedom of India. 480pp. 5⅜ x 8½. (Available in U.S. only.) 24593-4

CELTIC MYTHS AND LEGENDS, T. W. Rolleston. Masterful retelling of Irish and Welsh stories and tales. Cuchulain, King Arthur, Deirdre, the Grail, many more. First paperback edition. 58 full-page illustrations. 512pp. 5⅜ x 8½. 26507-2

THE PRINCIPLES OF PSYCHOLOGY, William James. Famous long course complete, unabridged. Stream of thought, time perception, memory, experimental methods; great work decades ahead of its time. 94 figures. 1,391pp. 5⅜ x 8½. 2-vol. set.
Vol. I: 20381-6 Vol. II: 20382-4

THE WORLD AS WILL AND REPRESENTATION, Arthur Schopenhauer. Definitive English translation of Schopenhauer's life work, correcting more than 1,000 errors, omissions in earlier translations. Translated by E. F. J. Payne. Total of 1,269pp. 5⅜ x 8½. 2-vol. set. Vol. 1: 21761-2 Vol. 2: 21762-0

MAGIC AND MYSTERY IN TIBET, Madame Alexandra David-Neel. Experiences among lamas, magicians, sages, sorcerers, Bonpa wizards. A true psychic discovery. 32 illustrations. 321pp. 5⅜ x 8½. (Available in U.S. only.) 22682-4

THE EGYPTIAN BOOK OF THE DEAD, E. A. Wallis Budge. Complete reproduction of Ani's papyrus, finest ever found. Full hieroglyphic text, interlinear transliteration, word-for-word translation, smooth translation. 533pp. 6½ x 9¼. 21866-X

MATHEMATICS FOR THE NONMATHEMATICIAN, Morris Kline. Detailed, college-level treatment of mathematics in cultural and historical context, with numerous exercises. Recommended Reading Lists. Tables. Numerous figures. 641pp. 5⅜ x 8½. 24823-2

PROBABILISTIC METHODS IN THE THEORY OF STRUCTURES, Isaac Elishakoff. Well-written introduction covers the elements of the theory of probability from two or more random variables, the reliability of such multivariable structures, the theory of random function, Monte Carlo methods of treating problems incapable of exact solution, and more. Examples. 502pp. 5⅜ x 8½. 40691-1

THE RIME OF THE ANCIENT MARINER, Gustave Doré, S. T. Coleridge. Doré's finest work; 34 plates capture moods, subtleties of poem. Flawless full-size reproductions printed on facing pages with authoritative text of poem. "Beautiful. Simply beautiful."–Publisher's Weekly. 77pp. 9¼ x 12. 22305-1

NORTH AMERICAN INDIAN DESIGNS FOR ARTISTS AND CRAFTSPEOPLE, Eva Wilson. Over 360 authentic copyright-free designs adapted from Navajo blankets, Hopi pottery, Sioux buffalo hides, more. Geometrics, symbolic figures, plant and animal motifs, etc. 128pp. 8⅜ x 11. (Not for sale in the United Kingdom.) 25341-4

SCULPTURE: Principles and Practice, Louis Slobodkin. Step-by-step approach to clay, plaster, metals, stone; classical and modern. 253 drawings, photos. 255pp. 8⅛ x 11. 22960-2

THE INFLUENCE OF SEA POWER UPON HISTORY, 1660–1783, A. T. Mahan. Influential classic of naval history and tactics still used as text in war colleges. First paperback edition. 4 maps. 24 battle plans. 640pp. 5⅜ x 8½. 25509-3

CATALOG OF DOVER BOOKS

THE STORY OF THE TITANIC AS TOLD BY ITS SURVIVORS, Jack Winocour (ed.). What it was really like. Panic, despair, shocking inefficiency, and a little heroism. More thrilling than any fictional account. 26 illustrations. 320pp. 5⅜ x 8½. 20610-6

FAIRY AND FOLK TALES OF THE IRISH PEASANTRY, William Butler Yeats (ed.). Treasury of 64 tales from the twilight world of Celtic myth and legend: "The Soul Cages," "The Kildare Pooka," "King O'Toole and his Goose," many more. Introduction and Notes by W. B. Yeats. 352pp. 5⅜ x 8½. 26941-8

BUDDHIST MAHAYANA TEXTS, E. B. Cowell and others (eds.). Superb, accurate translations of basic documents in Mahayana Buddhism, highly important in history of religions. The Buddha-karita of Asvaghosha, Larger Sukhavativyuha, more. 448pp. 5⅜ x 8½. 25552-2

ONE TWO THREE . . . INFINITY: Facts and Speculations of Science, George Gamow. Great physicist's fascinating, readable overview of contemporary science: number theory, relativity, fourth dimension, entropy, genes, atomic structure, much more. 128 illustrations. Index. 352pp. 5⅜ x 8½. 25664-2

EXPERIMENTATION AND MEASUREMENT, W. J. Youden. Introductory manual explains laws of measurement in simple terms and offers tips for achieving accuracy and minimizing errors. Mathematics of measurement, use of instruments, experimenting with machines. 1994 edition. Foreword. Preface. Introduction. Epilogue. Selected Readings. Glossary. Index. Tables and figures. 128pp. 5⅜ x 8½. 40451-X

DALÍ ON MODERN ART: The Cuckolds of Antiquated Modern Art, Salvador Dalí. Influential painter skewers modern art and its practitioners. Outrageous evaluations of Picasso, Cézanne, Turner, more. 15 renderings of paintings discussed. 44 calligraphic decorations by Dalí. 96pp. 5⅜ x 8½. (Available in U.S. only.) 29220-7

ANTIQUE PLAYING CARDS: A Pictorial History, Henry René D'Allemagne. Over 900 elaborate, decorative images from rare playing cards (14th–20th centuries): Bacchus, death, dancing dogs, hunting scenes, royal coats of arms, players cheating, much more. 96pp. 9¼ x 12¼. 29265-7

MAKING FURNITURE MASTERPIECES: 30 Projects with Measured Drawings, Franklin H. Gottshall. Step-by-step instructions, illustrations for constructing handsome, useful pieces, among them a Sheraton desk, Chippendale chair, Spanish desk, Queen Anne table and a William and Mary dressing mirror. 224pp. 8⅛ x 11¼. 29338-6

THE FOSSIL BOOK: A Record of Prehistoric Life, Patricia V. Rich et al. Profusely illustrated definitive guide covers everything from single-celled organisms and dinosaurs to birds and mammals and the interplay between climate and man. Over 1,500 illustrations. 760pp. 7½ x 10⅛. 29371-8

Paperbound unless otherwise indicated. Available at your book dealer, online at **www.doverpublications.com**, or by writing to Dept. GI, Dover Publications, Inc., 31 East 2nd Street, Mineola, NY 11501. For current price information or for free catalogues (please indicate field of interest), write to Dover Publications or log on to **www.doverpublications.com** and see every Dover book in print. Dover publishes more than 500 books each year on science, elementary and advanced mathematics, biology, music, art, literary history, social sciences, and other areas.